Making of America

CONCORD DAYS

Amos Bronson Alcott

HathiTrust
M Library

Distributed by

APPLEWOOD BOOKS
Carlisle, Massachusetts

Concord Days was originally published in 1872.

ISBN: 978-1-4585-0501-9

Making of America

For more information about this edition,
please contact:
The University of Michigan Libraries
Ann Arbor, MI 48109
or
Applewood Books
P.O. Box 27
Carlisle, MA 01741

Prepared for Publication by HP

CONCORD DAYS.

QUI LEGIT REGIT

CONCORD DAYS

BY

A. BRONSON ALCOTT

"Cheerful and various thoughts not always bound
To counsel, nor in deep ideas drowned."
JAMES HOWEL.

BOSTON
ROBERTS BROTHERS
1872.

Stereotyped and Printed by
ALFRED MUDGE & SON, BOSTON.

CONTENTS.

APRIL.

MAY.

APRIL.

1869.

"Now fades the last long streak of snow."
— *Tennyson.*

CONCORD DAYS.

DIARIES.

COME again into my study, having sat some time for greater comfort in the sunnier east room by an open fire, as needful in our climate, almost, as in that of changeable England. Busy days these last, with a little something to show for them. After all, I am here most at home, and myself surrounded by friendly pictures and books, free to follow the mood of the moment, — read, write, recreate. I wish more came of it all. Here are these voluminous diaries, showy seen from without, with far too little of life transcribed within. Was it the accident of being shown, when a boy, in the old oaken cabinet, my mother's little journal, that set me out in this chase of myself, continued almost uninterruptedly, and now fixed by habit as a part of the day, like the rising and setting of the sun? Yet it has educated me into whatever skill I possess with the pen, I know not to how much besides; has made me emulous of attaining the art of portraying my thoughts, occupations, surroundings, friendships; and could I succeed in sketching to the life a single day's doings, should esteem myself as having accomplished the chiefest feat in literature. Yet the nobler the life and the busier, the less, perhaps, gets written, and that which is, the less rewards perusal.

> "Life's the true poem could it be writ,
> Yet who can live at once and utter it."

All is in the flowing moments. But who shall arrest these and fix the features of the passing person behind the pageantry, and write the diary of one's existence?

MY HOUSE.

SATURDAY, 3.

MY neighbors flatter me in telling me that I have one of the best placed and most picturesque houses in our town. I know very well the secret of what they praise. 'T is simply adapting the color and repairs to the architecture, and holding these in keeping with the spot.

A house, like a person, invites by amiable reserves, as if it loved to be introduced in perspective and reached by courteous approaches. Let it show bashfully behind shrubberies, screen its proportions decorously in plain tints, not thrust itself rudely, like an inn, upon the street at cross-roads. A wide lawn in front, sloping to the road gracefully, gives it the stately air and courtly approach. I like the ancient mansions for this reason ; these old Puritan residences for their unpretending air, their sober tints, in strict keeping with Wordsworth's rule of coloring, viz. that of the sod about the grounds. A slight exaltation of this defines best the architecture by distinguishing it from surrounding objects in the landscape. Modest tints are always becoming. White and red intolerable. And for some variety in dressing, the neighboring barks of shrubbery suggest and best characterize the coloring.

As for fences and gates, I was told that mine were unlike any other in the world, yet as good as anybody's, hereby meaning to praise them, I infer. If less durable than others, the cost is inconsiderable, and has the associated pleasure, besides, of having come out of such ideal capital as I had invested in my own head and hands. A common carpenter would have spent more time in planing and fixing his pickets and set something in straight lines with angular corners to deform the landscape ; then the painter must have followed with some tint mixed neither by nature nor art. Now my work delights my eyes whenever I step out-of-doors, adding its ornament to the spot. Grotesque it may be with its knotted ornaments, Druid supports, yet in keeping with the woods behind it. Besides, what pleasure the construction has given! Form, color, ornamentation alike concern builder and occupant, as they were blos-

soms of his taste and of the landscape. A good architect is both builder and colorist, and should be a good
man besides, according to the ancient authorities.
Roman Vitruvius claims as much, if not more, of
him : —

" It is necessary," he says, " that an architect should
be instructed in the precepts of moral philosophy ; for
he ought to have a great soul, and be bold without
arrogance, just, faithful, and totally exempt from
avarice. He should have a great docility, which may
hinder him from neglecting the advice that is given
him, not only of the meanest artist, but also of those
that understand nothing of architecture ; for not only
architects but all the world must judge his works."

Houses have their history, are venerable on account
of their age and origin. Even our newly-settled country of but a century or two has already crowned homesteads still standing with royal honors. Mine, I conjecture, is not far from one hundred and fifty years'
standing. It was a first-class country house in its day,
with its window-seats in parlor and chambers, ornamental summers and casements, its ample fireplaces,
and lean-to on the northern side. Like most of its
period it was open to the road with overshadowing elms
still embowering the mansion ; had a lion-headed door-
knocker, and huge chimney-tops surmounting the gables.
Of learned ancestry, moreover ; having been the homestead of a brother of President Hoar, of Harvard College,
and remained in possession of members of that venerable

family down to near the beginning of the present century. The site is hardly surpassed by any on the old Boston road; the woods behind crowning the range of hills running north almost to the village, and bordering east on Wayside, Hawthorne's last residence. It must have been chosen by an original settler, probably coming with the Rev. Peter Bulkeley from England, in 1635.*

The ancient elms before the house, of a hundred years' standing and more, are the pride of the yard. It were sacrilege to remove a limb or twig unless decayed, so luxuriant and far-spreading, overshadowing the roof and gables, yet admitting the light into hall and chambers. Sunny rooms, sunny household. "Build your house," says a mystic author, "upon a firm foundation, and let your aspect be towards the east, where the sun rises, that so you may enjoy its fruitfulness in your household and orchards."

Whether the first settler planted these elms, or whether they are survivors of the primitive forest which was felled to make way and room for the rude shelter of the hardy settlers, is not ascertained. Their roots penetrate primitive soil; the surrounding grounds have become productive by the industry and skill, mellowed and meliorated by the humanities of their descendants. They came honestly by their homesteads, paying their swarthy claimants fair prices for

---

* Johnson, in his "Wonder Working Providence Concerning New England," describes the company of settlers on their way from Cambridge, under the lead of the Rev. Peter Bulkeley, the principal founder of Concord.

them; the landscape is still inviting by its prairie aspects, its brook-sides and meadows where the red men trod.

It was these broad meadows beside the "Grass ground River" that tempted alike the white and red man, — the one for pasturage, the other for fishing, — and brought the little colony through the wilderness to form the settlement named "Musketaquid," after the river of that name (signifying grass ground), and later taking that of Concord, not without note in history.

> "Beneath low hills, in the broad interval
> Through which at will our Indian rivulet
> Winds mindful still of sannup and of squaw,
> Whose pipe and arrow oft the plough unburies;
> Here, in pine houses, built of new-fallen trees,
> Supplanters of the tribe, the planters dwelt."

The view from the rustic seat overlooking my house commands the amphitheatre in which the house stands, and through which flows Mill brook, bordered on the south and east by the Lincoln woods. It is a quiet prospect and might be taken for an English landscape; needs but a tower or castle overtopping the trees surrounding it. The willows by the rock bridge over the brook, the winding lane once the main track of travel before the turnpike branching off from the old Boston road by Emerson's door was built, adds to the illusion, while on the east stands the pine-clad hill, Hawthorne's favorite haunt, and hiding his last residence from sight.

On the southwest is an ancient wood, Thoreau's pride, beyond which is Walden Pond, distant about a mile from my house, and best reached by the lane opening opposite Hawthorne's. Fringed on all sides by woods, the interval, once a mill pond, is now in meadow and garden land, the slopes planted in vineyards, market gardens and orchards lining the road along which stand the farmers' houses visible in the opening.

This road has more than a local interest. If any road may claim the originality of being entitled to the name of American, it is this, — since along its dust the British regulars retreated from their memorable repulse at the Old North Bridge, the Concord military following fast upon their heels, and from the hill-tops giving them salutes of musketry till they disappeared beyond Lexington, and gave a day to history.

An agricultural town from the first, it is yet such in large measure; though like others in its neighborhood becoming suburban and commercial. Fields once in corn and grass are now in vineyards and orchards, tillage winding up the slopes from the low lands to the hill-tops. The venerable woods once crowning these are fast falling victims to the axe. The farmsteads are no longer the rural homes they were when every member of the family took part in domestic affairs; foreign help serves where daughters once served; they with their brothers having left the housekeeping and farming for school, factories, trade, a profession, and things are drifting towards an urbane and municipal civilization, the metropolis extending its boundaries, and absorbing the townships for many miles round.

Moreover, the primitive features of the landscape are being obliterated by the modern facilities for business and travel, less perhaps than in most places lying so near the metropolis; the social still less than the natural; the descendants of the primitive fathers of the settlement cherishing a pride of ancestry not unbecoming in a republic, less favorable for the perpetuation of family distinctions and manners than in countries under monarchical rule.

OUTLOOK.

MONDAY, 5.

ONE'S outlook is a part of his virtue. Does it matter nothing to him what objects accost him whenever he glances from his windows, or steps out-of-doors? He who is so far weaned from the landscape, or indifferent to it, as not to derive a sweet and robust habit of character therefrom, seems out of keeping with nature and himself. I suspect something amiss in him who has no love, no enthusiasm for his surroundings, and that his friendships, if such he profess, are of a cold and isolate quality at best; one even questions, at times, whether the residents of cities, where art has thrown around them a world of its own, are compensated by all this luxury of display, — to say nothing of the social artifices wont to steal into their costly compliments, — for the simple surroundings of the countryman, which prompt to manliness and true gentility. A country dwelling without shrubbery, hills near or in the distance, a forest and water view, if but a rivulet, seems so far incomplete as if the occupants themselves were raw and impoverished. Wood and water god both, man loves to traverse the forests, wade the streams, and confess his kindred alliance with primeval things. He leaps not from the woods into civility at a single bound, neither comes from cities and conversations freed from the wildness of his dispositions. Something of the forester stirs within him when occasion provokes, as if men were trees transformed, and delighted to claim their affinities with their sylvan ancestry.

> Man never tires of Nature's scene,
> Himself the liveliest evergreen.

THOREAU.

My friend and neighbor united these qualities of sylvan and human in a more remarkable manner than any whom it has been my happiness to know. Lover of the wild, he lived a borderer on the confines of civilization, jealous of the least encroachment upon his possessions.

> "Society were all but rude
> In his umbrageous solitude."

I had never thought of knowing a man so thoroughly of the country, and so purely a son of nature. I think he had the profoundest passion for it of any one of his time ; and had the human sentiment been as tender and pervading, would have given us pastorals of which Virgil and Theocritus might have envied him the authorship had they chanced to be his contemporaries. As it was, he came nearer the antique spirit than any of our native poets, and touched the fields and groves and streams of his native town with a classic interest that shall not fade. Some of his verses are suffused with an elegiac tenderness, as if the woods and brooks bewailed the absence of their Lycidas, and murmured their griefs meanwhile to one another, — responsive like idyls. Living in close companionship with nature, his muse breathed the spirit and voice of poetry. For when the heart is once divorced from the senses and all sympathy with common things, then poetry has fled and the love that sings.

The most welcome of companions was this plain countryman. One seldom meets with thoughts like his, coming so scented of mountain and field breezes and rippling springs, so like a luxuriant clod from under forest leaves, moist and mossy with earth-spirits. His presence was tonic, like ice-water in dog-days to the parched citizen pent in chambers and under brazen ceilings. Welcome as the gurgle of brooks and dipping of pitchers, — then drink and be cool ! He seemed one with things, of nature's essence and core, knit of strong timbers, — like a wood and its inhabitants. There was in him sod and shade, wilds and waters manifold, — the mould and mist of earth and sky. Self-poised and sagacious as any denizen of the elements, he had the key to every animal's brain, every plant; and were an Indian to flower forth and reveal the scents hidden in his cranium, it would not be more surprising than the speech of our Sylvanus. He belonged to the Homeric age, — was older than pastures and gardens, as if he were of the race of heroes and one with the elements. He of all men seemed to be the native New-Englander, as much so as the oak, the granite ledge; our best sample of an indigenous American, untouched by the old country, unless he came down rather from Thor, the Northman, whose name he bore.

A peripatetic philosopher, and out-of-doors for the best part of his days and nights, he had manifold weather and seasons in him; the manners of an animal of probity and virtue unstained. Of all our moralists, he seemed the wholesomest, the busiest, and the best republican citizen in the world; always at home minding his own affairs. A little over-confident by genius, and stiffly individual, dropping society clean out of his theories, while standing friendly in his strict sense of friendship, there was in him an integrity and love of justice that made possible and actual the virtues of Sparta and the Stoics, — all the more welcome in his time of shuffling and pusillanimity. Plutarch

would have made him immortal in his pages had he
lived before his day.   Nor have we any so modern
withal, so entirely his own and ours : too purely so to be
appreciated at once.   A scholar by birthright, and an
author, his fame had not, at his decease, travelled far
from the banks of the rivers he described in his books ;
but one hazards only the truth in affirming of his prose,
that in substance and pith, it surpasses that of any
naturalist of his time ; and he is sure of large reading in
the future.   There are fairer fishes in his pages than
any swimming in our streams ; some sleep of his
on the banks of the Merrimack by moonlight that
Egypt never rivalled ; a morning of which Memnon
might have envied the music, and a greyhound he once
had, meant for Adonis ; frogs, better than any of
Aristophanes ; apples wilder than Adam's.   His
senses seemed double, giving him access to secrets not
easily read by others ; in sagacity resembling that of
the beaver, the bee, the dog, the deer ; an instinct
for seeing and judging, as by some other, or seventh
sense ; dealing with objects as if they were shooting
forth from his mind mythologically, thus completing
the world all round to his senses ; a creation of his at
the moment.   I am sure he knew the animals one by
one, as most else knowable in his town ; the plants,
the geography, as Adam did in his Paradise, if,
indeed, he were not that ancestor himself.   His
works are pieces of exquisite sense, celebrations of
Nature's virginity exemplified by rare learning, deli-

cate art, replete with observations as accurate as original; contributions of the unique to the natural history of his country, and without which it were incomplete. Seldom has a head circumscribed so much of the sense and core of Cosmos as this footed intelligence.

If one would learn the wealth of wit there was in this plain man, the information, the poetry, the piety, he should have accompanied him on an afternoon walk to Walden, or elsewhere about the skirts of his village residence. Pagan as he might outwardly appear, yet he was the hearty worshipper of whatsoever is sound and wholesome in nature, — a piece of russet probity and strong sense, that nature delighted to own and honor. His talk was suggestive, subtle, sincere, under as many masks and mimicries as the shows he might pass; as significant, substantial, — nature choosing to speak through his mouth-piece, — cynically, perhaps, and searching into the marrows of men and times he spoke of, to his discomfort mostly and avoidance.

Nature, poetry, life, — not politics, not strict science, not society as it is, — were his preferred themes. The world was holy, the things seen symbolizing the things unseen, and thus worthy of worship, calling men out-of-doors and under the firmament for health and wholesomeness to be insinuated into their souls, not as idolators, but as idealists. His religion was of the most primitive type, inclusive of all natural creatures and things, even to " the sparrow that falls to the ground," though never by shot of his, and for whatsoever was manly in men, his worship was comparable to that of the priests and heroes of all time. I should say he inspired the sentiment of love, if, indeed, the sentiment did not seem to partake of something purer, were that possible, but nameless from its excellency. Certainly he was better poised and more nearly self-reliant than other men.

> " The happy man who lived content
> With his own town, his continent,
> Whose chiding streams its banks did curb
> As ocean circumscribes its orb,
> Round which, when he his walk did take,
> Thought he performed far more than Drake;
> For other lands he took less thought
> Than this his muse and mother brought."

More primitive and Homeric than any American, his style of thinking was robust, racy, as if Nature herself had built his sentences and seasoned the sense of his paragraphs with her own vigor and salubrity. Nothing can be spared from them; there is nothing superfluous; all is compact, concrete, as nature is.

His politics were of a piece with his individualism. We must admit that he found little in political or religious establishments answering to his wants, that his attitude was defiant, if not annihilating, as if he had said to himself: —

" The state is man's pantry at most, and filled at an enormous cost, — a spoliation of the human commonwealth. Let it go. Heroes can live on nuts, and freemen sun themselves in the clefts of rocks, rather than sell their liberty for this pottage of slavery. We, the few honest neighbors, can help one another ; and should the state ask any favors of us, we can take the matter into consideration leisurely, and at our convenience give a respectful answer.

" But why require a state to protect one's rights? the man is all. Let him husband himself; needs he other servant or runner? Self-keeping is the best economy. That is a great age when the state is nothing and man is all. He founds himself in freedom, and maintains his uprightness therein ; founds an empire and maintains states. Just retire from those concerns, and see how soon they must needs go to pieces, the sooner for the virtue thus withdrawn from them. All the manliness of individuals is sunk in that partnership in trade. Not only must I come out of institutions, but come out of myself, if I will be free and independent. Shall one be denied the privilege on coming of mature age of choosing whether he will be a citizen of the country he happens to be born in, or another? And what better title to a spot of ground than being a man, and having none? Is not man superior to state or country? I plead exemption from all interference by men or states with my individual prerogatives. That is mine which none can steal from me, nor is that yours which I or any man can take away."

> " I am too high born to be propertied,
>   To be a secondary at control,
>   Or useful serving man and instrument
>   To any sovereign state throughout the world."

A famous speech is recorded of an old Norseman thoroughly characteristic of this Teuton. " I believe neither in idols nor demons ; I put my sole trust in my own strength of body and soul." The ancient crest of a pick-axe, with the motto, " Either I will find a way or make one," characterizes the same sturdy independence and practical materialism which distinguishes the descendants of Thor, whose symbol was a hammer.

He wrote in his Journal : —

" Perhaps I am descended from the Northman named Thorer, the dog-footed. He was the most powerful man of the North. To judge from his name, *Thorer Hund* belonged to the same family. Thorer is one of the most, if not the most common name in the chronicles of the Northmen. Snörro Sturleson says, ' from Thor's name comes Thorer, also Thorarimnn.' Again, ' Earl Rognvald was King Harald's dearest friend, and the king had the greatest regard for him. He was married to Hilda, a daughter of Rolf Nalfia, and their sons were Rolf and Thorer. Rolf became a great Viking, and of so stout a growth that no horse could carry him, and wheresoever he went, he went on foot, and therefore he was called Gange-Rolf.' Laing says in a note, what Sturleson also tells in the text, ' Gange-Rolf, Rolf-Ganger, Rolf the walker, was the conqueror of Normandy. Gange-Rolf's son was William, father of Richard, who was the father of Richard Longspear, and grandfather of William the Bastard, from whom the following English kings are descended.' "

"King Harald set Earl Rognvald's son Thorer over Möre, and gave him his daughter Alof in marriage. Thorer, called the Silent, got the same territory his father Rognvald had possessed. His brother Einar going into battle to take vengeance on his father's murderers, sang a kind of reproach against his brothers, Rollang and Rolf, for their slowness, and concludes :—

> ' And silent Thorer sits and dreams
>   At home, beside the mead bowl's streams.'

"Of himself it is related, that ' he cut a spread eagle on the back of his enemy Halfdan.'

"So it seems that from one branch of the family were descended the kings of England, and from the other, myself."

In his journal I find these lines : —

> "Light-headed, thoughtless, shall I take my way
>   When I to Thee this being have resigned ;
>   Well knowing when upon a future day,
>   With usurer's trust, more than myself to find."

NOTE. "Thoreau was born in Concord on the 12th of July, 1817. The old-fashioned house, its roof nearly reaching to the ground in the rear, remains as it was when he first saw the light in the easternmost of its upper chambers. It was the residence of his grandmother, and a perfect piece of our New-England style of building, with its gray, unpainted boards, its grassy, unfenced door-yard. The house is somewhat isolate and remote from thoroughfares. The Virginia road is an old-fashioned, winding, at length deserted pathway, the more smiling for its forked orchards, tumbling walks, and mossy banks. About the house are pleasant, sunny meadows, deep with their beds of peat, so cheering with its homely, heath-like fragrance, and in its front runs a constant stream through the centre of that great tract sometimes called ' Bedford Levels,' — this brook a source of the Shawsheen

River. It was lovely that he should draw his first breath in a pure country air, out of crowded towns, amid the pleasant russet fields.

"His parents were active, vivacious people; his grandfather, by his father's side, coming from the Isle of Jersey, a Frenchman and Catholic, who married a Scotch woman named Jennie Burns. On his mother's side the descent is from the well-known Jones family of Weston, Mass., and the Rev. Charles Dunbar, a graduate of Harvard College, who preached in Salem, and at length settled in Keene, New Hampshire. As variable an ancestry as can well be afforded, with marked family characters on both sides. About a year and a half from Henry's birth, the family removed to the town of Chelmsford, thence to Boston, coming back, however, to Concord when he was of a very tender age; his earliest memory of most of the town was a ride to Walden Pond with his grandmother, when he thought that he should be glad to live there. He retained a peculiar pronunciation of the letter R, with a decided French accent. He says, 'September is the fifth month with a burr in it.' His great-grandmother's name was Marie le Galais, and his grandfather, John Thoreau, was baptized April 28, 1754, and partook of the Catholic sacrament in the parish of St. Helier, Isle of Jersey, in May, 1773. Thus near to old France and the church was our Yankee boy.

"A moment may be spent on a few traits of Thoreau, of a personal kind. In height he was about the average. In his build, spare, with limbs that were rather longer than usual, or of which he made a longer use. His face once seen could not be forgotten; the features quite marked, the nose aquiline, or very Roman, like one of the portraits of Cæsar (more like a beak, as was said), large overhanging brows above the deepest-set blue eyes that could be seen, — blue in certain lights, and in others gray, — eyes expressive of all shades of feeling, but never weak or near-sighted; the forehead not unusually broad or high, full of concentrated energy and purpose; the mouth, with prominent lips, pursed up with meaning and thought when shut, and giving out when open a stream of the most varied and unusual and instructive sayings. His hair was a dark brown, exceedingly abundant, fine, and soft, and for several years he wore a comely beard. His whole figure had an active earnestness as if he had not a moment to waste. The clenched hand betokened purpose. In walking he made a short cut if he could, and when sitting in the shade, or by the wall-side, seemed merely the clearer to look forward into the next piece of activity. Even in the boat he had a wary, transitory air, his eyes on the lookout; perhaps there might be ducks, or the Blondin turtle, or an otter, or sparrow. He was a plain man in his features and dress, — one who could not be mistaken, and this kind of plainness is not out of keeping with beauty. He sometimes went as far as homeliness, which again, even if there be a prejudice against it, shines out at times beyond a vulgar beauty."

W. ELLERY CHANNING.

SELF–PRIVACY.

THURSDAY, 8.

" A sweet self-privacy in a right soul
  Outruns the earth, and lines the utmost pole."

FOR a diary, slight arches will suffice to convey the day's freight across ; the lighter these, the speedier and more graceful the transit. Any current event, passing thought, rumor, were transportable, if simply dispatched. And the more significant, as the more familiar and private. Life were the less sweet and companionable if cumbered with affairs, overloaded with thought, dizzied with anxieties. Better the quiet temper that takes the days as they pass, and as if an eternity were vouchsafed for completing one's task, the time too short to waste in murmurs or postponements.

" Cares, like eclipses, darken our endeavors ;
  Our duties are our best gods."

A quiet life furnishes little of incident ; dealing with thoughts and things in a meditative manner, it has the less for those who have a more stirring stake in current affairs. Yet one fancies that what interests himself may interest others of like mind, if not of like pursuits ; and more especially when, as in a diary, he writes only of what has some real or imagined relation to what concerns him. His record may be careless, inconsequent, like the days it chronicles, with but the slender thread of sleep connecting its leaves; or perhaps the newspaper, once an accident, and coming irregularly, links his evening with morning, morning with evening; newspaper before breakfast, before business, before sleep; daily bread. One almost defines his culture, his social standing, by the journals he takes. Observe the difference between persons and neighborhoods familiar with current newspapers and those who are not. Very different from the times when a country boy must ride his miles after his Saturday's work to get some glimmering of what was passing in the great world around him; before libraries and lectures were established, steam and lightning were carriers and couriers for all mankind. No life is insular now. Every thought resounds throughout the globe. Electricity competes with thought in the race. The telegraph, locomotive, the press, render cabinets and colleges almost superfluous. Travel makes all men countrymen, makes people noblemen and kings, every man tasting of liberty and dominion. And who but the kings themselves can unking themselves?

Still, like most things, our periodical literature is far from being a pure benefit, and one may quote Plato's saying as applicable to the superficial culture which this of itself fosters: " Total ignorance were in no wise a thing so vile and wicked, nor the greatest of evils; but multifarious knowledge and learning acquired under bad management, causes much more harm."

Rather what is thought and spoken in drawing-rooms, clubs, in private assemblies, best intimates the spirit and tendencies of a community. Things are known but at second-hand as represented in public prints, or spoken on platforms. Admitted to private houses, one may report accurately the census of civility, and cast the horoscope of the coming time. Nor do I sympathize with some of my friends in their dislike of reporters. One defends himself from intrusion, as a general rule; but where the public have a generous interest in one's thoughts, his occupations and manners, the discourtesy is rather in withholding these from any false modesty. Besides, the version is more likely to be nearer the truth than if left to chance curiosity, which piques itself all the more on getting what was thus withheld, with any additions the mood favors.

SUNDAY LECTURES.

SUNDAY, 11.

THE course of Sunday lectures at Horticultural Hall opened in January closes to-day. They have proved a brilliant success. Each speaker has attracted, besides the body of steady attendants, his personal friends, thus varying the audiences from Sunday to Sunday, and giving an example of varied teaching unprecedented in our time. The reports of these discourses, imperfect as they are, deserve preservation. They have relation to the drift of thinking in our New-England community especially, and are of historical importance. If not accepting all that has been spoken on this platform by the successive speakers, one may take a hearty interest in these adventures into the world of thought and duty; nor can any who have attended steadily from Sunday to Sunday question their serving a religious need of the time. The views of persons, distinguished as are most of the speakers, are not insignificant, since these are not among the least of the influences secretly, if not openly, moulding the manners and institutions of a community in which the thoughts and aims of the humblest individuals have weight, and the young are so eager to learn of their thoughtful elders.

When I recollect the ardor with which I sought the acquaintance of those whom I imagined had ideas to communicate, and my delight in such when found, I am led to think how very desirable were an institution to which young students might resort during such portion of the year as might be most convenient, to enjoy the fellowship of some of our most cultivated persons, — scholarships being provided for such as had not the means of defraying the necessary expenses, — thus enabling bright young men and women, whether college graduates or not, to complete what colleges do not give. Not every student comes into that intellectual sympathy with his professor, which renders instruction most enjoyable, yet without which the highest ends of culture are not attained. With a faculty composed of persons whose names a moment's thought will suggest, opportunities would be given for that sympathetic communion of mind with mind in which all living instruction and influence consist.

EMERSON.

TUESDAY, 13.

EMERSON has lately completed a course of readings on English Poetry to an appreciative company in Boston. It is a variation of his method of communicating with his companies, and not less becoming than even his usual form of lecture. It matters not in his case; for such is the charm of his manner, that wherever he appears, the cultured class will delight in his utterances; and one may quote Socrates in Phædrus, where Plato makes him say, " For as men lead hungry creatures by holding out a green bough, or an apple, so you, Phædrus, it would seem, might lead me about all Attica, and, indeed, wherever else you please, by extending to me discourses out of your books." Not less aptly Goethe describes him, in his letters to Schiller, where he calls the rhapsodist, "A wise man, who, in calm thoughtfulness, shows what has happened; his discourse aiming less to excite than to calm his auditors, in order that they shall listen to him with contentment and long. He apportions the interest equally, because it is not in his power to balance a too lively impression.

2

He grasps backwards and forwards at pleasure. He is followed, because he has only to do with the imagination, which of itself produces images, and which, up to a certain degree, is indifferent what kind he calls up. He does not appear to his auditors, but recites, as it were, behind a curtain ; so there is a total abstraction from himself, and it seems to them as though they heard only the voice of the Muses."

See our Ion standing there, his audience, his manuscript before him, himself also an auditor, as he reads, of the Genius sitting behind him, and to whom he defers, eagerly catching the words, — the words, — as if the accents were first reaching his ears too, and entrancing alike oracle and auditor. We admire the stately sense, the splendor of diction, and are charmed as we listen. Even his hesitancy between the delivery of his periods, his perilous passages from paragraph to paragraph of manuscript, we have almost learned to like, as if he were but sorting his keys meanwhile for opening his cabinets ; the spring of locks following, himself seeming as eager as any of us to get sight of his specimens as they come forth from their proper drawers, and we wait willingly till his gem is out glittering ; admire the setting, too, scarcely less than the jewel itself. The magic minstrel and speaker, whose rhetoric, voiced as by organ-stops, delivers the sentiment from his breast in cadences peculiar to himself ; now hurling it forth on the ear, echoing ; then, as his mood and matter invite, dying away, like

" Music of mild lutes,
Or silver-coated flutes,
Or the concealing winds that can convey
Never their tone to the rude ear of day."

He works his miracles with it, as Hermes did, his voice conducting the sense alike to eye and ear by its lyrical movement and refraining melody. So his compositions affect us, not as logic linked in syllogisms, but as voluntaries rather, as preludes, in which one is not tied to any design of air, but may vary his key or note at pleasure, as if improvised without any particular scope of argument; each period, paragraph, being a perfect note in itself, however it may chance chime with its accompaniments in the piece, as a waltz of wandering stars, a dance of Hesperus with Orion. His rhetoric dazzles by its circuits, contrasts, antitheses; imagination, as in all sprightly minds, being his wand of Power. He comes along his own paths, too, and in his own fashion. What though he build his piers downwards from the firmament to the tumbling tides, and so throw his radiant span across the fissures of his argument, and himself pass over the frolic arches, Ariel-wise, — is the skill less admirable, the masonry the less secure for its singularity? So his books are best read as irregular writings, in which the sentiment is, by his enthusiasm, transfused throughout the piece, telling on the mind in cadences of a current undersong, giving the impression of a connected whole, — which it seldom is, — such is the rhapsodist's cunning in its structure and delivery.

The highest compliment we can pay the scholar is that of having edified and instructed us, we know not how, unless by the pleasure his words have given us. Conceive how much the lyceum owes to his presence and teachings ; how great the debt of many to him for their hour's entertainment. His, if any one's, let the institution pass into history, since his art, more than another's, has clothed it with beauty, and made it the place of popular resort, our purest organ of intellectual entertainment for New England and the Western cities. And besides this, its immediate value to his auditors everywhere, it has been serviceable in ways they least suspect ; most of his works, having had their first readings on its platform, were here fashioned and polished, in good part, like Plutarch's morals, to become the more acceptable to readers of his published books. Does it matter what topic he touches? He adorns all with a severe sententious beauty, a freshness and sanction next to that of godliness, if not that in spirit and effect.

> " The princely mind, that can
>   Teach man to keep a God in man ;
>   And when wise poets would search out to see
>   Good men, behold them all in thee."

'T is over thirty years since his first book was printed. Then followed volumes of essays, poems, orations, addresses ; and during all the intervening period, down to the present, he has read briefs of his lectures through a wide range, from Canada to the Capitol; in most of the Free States; in the large cities, East and West, before large audiences; in the smallest towns, and to the humblest companies. Such has been his appeal to the mind of his countrymen, such his acceptance by them. He has read lectures in the principal cities of England also. A poet, speaking to individuals as few others can speak, and to persons in their privileged moments, he is heard as none others are. The more personal he is, the more prevailing, if not the more popular. 'T is everything to have a true believer in the world, dealing with men and matters as if they were divine in idea and real in fact; meeting persons and events at a glance directly, not at a millionth remove, and so passing fair and fresh into life and literature.

Consider how largely our letters have been enriched by his contributions. Consider, too, the change his views have wrought in our methods of thinking; how he has won over the bigot, the unbeliever, at least to tolerance and moderation, if not acknowledgment, by his circumspection and candor of statement.

> " His shining armor,
> A perfect charmer;
> Even the hornets of divinity
> Allow him a brief space,
> And his thought has a place
> Upon the well-bound library's chaste shelves,
> Where man of various wisdom rarely delves."

Poet and moralist, he has beauty and truth for all men's edification and delight. His works are studies. And any youth of free senses and fresh affections shall be spared years of tedious toil, in which wisdom and fair learning are, for the most part, held at arm's-length, planets' width, from his grasp, by graduating from this college. His books are surcharged with vigorous thoughts, a sprightly wit. They abound in strong sense, happy humor, keen criticisms, subtile insights, noble morals, clothed in a chaste and manly diction, fresh with the breath of health and progress.

We characterize and class him with the moralists who surprise us with an accidental wisdom, strokes of wit, felicities of phrase, — as Plutarch, Seneca, Epictetus, Marcus Aurelius, Saadi, Montaigne, Bacon, Selden, Sir Thomas Browne, Cowley, Coleridge, Goethe, — with whose delightful essays, notwithstanding all the pleasure they give us, we still plead our disappointment at not having been admitted to the closer intimacy which these loyal leaves had with their owners' mind before torn from his note-books, jealous, even, at not having been taken into his confidence in the editing itself.

We read, never as if he were the dogmatist, but a fair-speaking mind, frankly declaring his convictions, and committing these to our consideration, hoping we may have thought like things ourselves; oftenest, indeed, taking this for granted as he wrote. There is nothing of the spirit of proselyting, but the delightful deference ever to our free sense and right of opinion.

He might take for his motto the sentiment of Henry More, where, speaking of himself, he says : " Exquisite disquisition begets diffidence ; diffidence in knowledge, humility ; humility, good manners and meek conversation. For my part, I desire no man to take anything I write or speak upon trust without canvassing, and would be thought rather to propound than to assert what I have here or elsewhere written or spoken. But continually to have expressed my diffidence in the very tractates and colloquies themselves, had been languid and ridiculous."

Then he has chosen proper times and manners for saying his good things; has spoken to almost every great interest as it rose. Nor has he let the good opportunities pass unheeded, or failed to make them for himself. He has taken discretion along as his constant attendant and ally ; has shown how the gentlest temper ever deals the surest blows. His method is that of the sun against his rival for the cloak, and so is free from any madness of those, who, forgetting the strength of the solar ray, go blustering against men's prejudices, as if the wearers would run at once against these winds of opposition into their arms for shelter. What higher praise can we bestow on any one than to say of him, that he harbors another's prejudices with a hospitality so cordial as to give him for the time the sympathy next best to, if, indeed, it be not edification in, charity itself? For what disturbs more, and distracts mankind, than the uncivil manners that cleave man from man? Yet, for whose amendment letters, love, Christianity, were all given !

There is a virtuous curiosity felt by readers of remarkable books to learn something more of their author's literary tastes, habits, and dispositions, than these ordinarily furnish. Yet to gratify this is a task as difficult as delicate, requiring a diffidency akin to that with which one would accost the author himself, and without which graceful armor it were impertinent for a friend even to undertake it. We may venture but a stroke or two here.

All men love the country who love mankind with a wholesome love, and have poetry and company in them. Our essayist makes good this preference. If city bred, he has been for the best part of his life a villager and countryman. Only a traveller at times professionally, he prefers home-keeping ; is a student of the landscape, of mankind, of rugged strength wherever found ; liking plain persons, plain ways, plain clothes ; prefers earnest people ; shuns egotists, publicity ; likes solitude, and knows its uses. Courting society as a spectacle not less than a pleasure, he carries off the spoils. Delighting in the broadest views of men and things, he seeks all accessible displays of both for draping his thoughts and works. And how is his page produced? Is it imaginable that he conceives his piece as a whole, and then sits down to execute his task at a heat? Is not this imaginable rather, and the key to the

construction of his works? Living for composition as
few authors can, and holding company, studies, sleep,
exercise, affairs, subservient to thought, his products
are gathered as they ripen, stored in his commonplaces;
their contents transcribed at intervals, and classified.
It is the order of ideas, of imagination observed in the
arrangement, not of logical sequence. You may begin
at the last paragraph and read backwards. 'T is Iris-
built. Each period is self-poised; there may be a
chasm of years between the opening passage and the
last written, and there is endless time in the composition. Jewels all! Separate stars. You may have
them in a galaxy, if you like, or view them separate
and apart. But every one finds that, if he take an
essay, or verses, however the writer may have pleased
himself with the cunning workmanship, 't is cloud-
fashioned, and a blind pathway for any one else.
Cross as you can, or not cross, it matters not, you may
climb or leap, move in circles, turn somersaults;

"In sympathetic sorrow sweep the ground,"

like his swallow in Hermione. Dissolving views, prospects, vistas opening wide and far, yet earth, sky, —
realities all, not illusions. Here is substance, sod, sun;
much fair weather in the seer as in his leaves. The
whole quaternion of the seasons, the sidereal year, has
been poured into these periods. Afternoon walks furnished their perspectives, rounded and melodized them.
These good things have been talked and slept over,

meditated standing and sitting, read and polished in the utterance, submitted to all various tests, and, so accepted, they pass into print. Light fancies, dreams, moods, refrains, were set on foot, and sent jaunting about the fields, along wood-paths, by Walden shores, by hill and brook-sides, to come home and claim their rank and honors too in his pages. Composed of surrounding matters, populous with thoughts, brisk with images, these books are wholesome, homelike, and could have been written only in New England, and by our poet.

> " Because I was content with these poor fields,
>   Low, open meads, slender and sluggish streams,
>   And found a home in haunts which others scorned,
>   The partial wood-gods overpaid my love,
>   And granted me the freedom of their state,
>   And in their secret senate have prevailed
>   With the dear, dangerous lords that rule our life,
>   Made moon and planets parties to their bond,
>   And through my rock-like, solitary wont
>   Shot million rays of thought and tenderness.
>   For me, in showers, in sweeping showers, the spring
>   Visits the valley; — break away the clouds, —
>   I bathe in the morn's soft and silvered air,
>   And loiter willing by yon loitering stream.
>   Sparrows far off, and nearer, April's bird,
>   Blue-coated, flying before from tree to tree,
>   Courageous, sing a delicate overture
>   To lead the tardy concert of the year.
>   Onward and nearer rides the sun of May;
>   And wide around, the marriage of the plants

Is sweetly solemnized.   Then flows amain
The surge of summer's beauty; dell and crag,
Hollow and lake, hill-side, and pine arcade,
Are touched with Genius.   Yonder ragged cliff
Has thousand faces in a thousand hours.

.   .   .   .   The gentle deities
Showed me the lore of colors and of sounds,
The innumerable tenements of beauty,
The miracle of generative force,
Far-reaching concords of astronomy
Felt in the plants and in the punctual birds;
Better, the linked purpose of the whole,
And, chiefest prize, found I true liberty
In the glad home plain-dealing nature gave.
The polite found me impolite; the great
Would mortify me, but in vain; for still
I am a willow of the wilderness,
Loving the wind that bent me.   All my hurts
My garden spade can heal.   A woodland walk,
A quest of river-grapes, a mocking thrush,
A wild-rose, or rock-loving columbine,
Salve my worst wounds.
For thus the wood-gods murmured in my ear:
' Dost love our manners?   Canst thou silent lie?
Canst thou, thy pride forgot, like nature pass
Into the winter night's extinguished mood?
Canst thou shine now, then darkle,
And being latent feel thyself no less?
As, when the all-worshipped moon attracts the eye,
The river, hill, stems, foliage, are obscure,
Yet envies none, none are unenviable.' "

I know of but one subtraction from the pleasure the

reading of his books — shall I say his conversation? —
gives me, — his pains to be impersonal or discrete, as
if he feared any the least intrusion of himself were an
offence offered to self-respect, the courtesy due to intercourse and authorship; thus depriving his page, his
company, of attractions the great masters of both knew
how to insinuate into their text and talk without over-
stepping the bounds of social or literary decorum.
What is more delightful than personal magnetism?
'T is the charm of good fellowship as of good writing.
To get and to give the largest measure of satisfaction,
to fill ourselves with the nectar of select experiences,
not without some intertinctures of egotism so charming
in a companion, is what we seek in books of the class
of his, as in their authors. We associate diffidence
properly with learning, frankness with fellowship, and
owe a certain blushing reverence to both. For though
our companion be a bashful man, — and he is the worse
if wanting this grace, — we yet wish him to be an
enthusiast behind all reserves, and capable of abandonment sometimes in his books. I know how rare this
genial humor is, this frankness of the blood, and how
surpassing are the gifts of good spirits, especially here
in cold New England, where, for the most part,

> " Our virtues grow
> Beneath our humors, and at seasons show."

And yet, under our east winds of reserve, there hides
an obscure courtesy in the best natures, which neither

temperament nor breeding can spoil. Sometimes manners the most distant are friendly foils for holding eager dispositions subject to the measures of right behavior. 'T is not every New-Englander that dares venture upon the frankness, the plain speaking, commended by the Greek poet.

> " Caress me not with words, while far away
> Thy heart is absent, and thy feelings stray;
> But if thou love me with a faithful breast,
> Be that pure love with zeal sincere exprest;
> And if thou hate, the bold aversion show
> With open face avowed, and known my foe."

Fortunate the visitor who is admitted of a morning for the high discourse, or permitted to join the poet in his afternoon walks to Walden, the cliffs, or elsewhere, — hours likely to be remembered as unlike any others in his calendar of experiences. I may say for me they have made ideas possible by hospitalities given to a fellowship so enjoyable. Shall I describe them as sallies oftenest into the cloud-lands, into scenes and intimacies ever new, none the less novel or remote than when first experienced, colloquies, in favored moments, on themes, perchance,

> " Of Fate, free-will, foreknowledge absolute;"

nor yet

> "In wand'ring mazes lost,"

as in Milton's page;

> But pathways plain through starry alcoves high,
> Or thence descending to the level plains.

Interviews, however, bringing their trail of perplexing thoughts, costing some days' duties, several nights' sleep oftentimes to restore one to his place and poise for customary employment; half a dozen annually being full as many as the stoutest heads may well undertake without detriment. Certainly safer not to venture without the sure credentials, unless one will have his pretensions pricked, his conceits reduced to their vague dimensions.

> " Fools have no means to meet
> But by their feet."

But to the modest, the ingenuous, the gifted, welcome! Nor can any bearing be more poetic and polite than his to all such, to youth and accomplished women especially. I may not intrude further than to say, that, beyond any I have known, his is a faith approaching to superstition concerning admirable persons, the divinity of friendship come down from childhood, and surviving yet in memory if not in expectation, the rumor of excellence of any sort being like the arrival of a new gift to mankind, and he the first to proffer his recognition and hope. His affection for conversation, for clubs, is a lively intimation of this religion of fellowship. He, shall we say, if any, must have taken the census of the admirable people of his time, perhaps numbering as many among his friends as most living Americans, while he is recognized as the representative mind of his country, to whom distinguished foreigners are especially commended on visiting us.

Of Emerson's books I am not here designing to speak critically, rather of his genius and personal influence; yet, in passing, may remark that his " English Traits " deserves to be honored as one in which England, Old and New, may alike take national pride as being the liveliest portraiture of British genius and accomplishments there is, — a book, like Tacitus, to be quoted as a masterpiece of historical painting, and perpetuating the New-Englander's fame with that of his race. 'T is a victory of eyes over hands, a triumph of ideas. Nor has there been for some time any criticism of a people so characteristic and complete. It remains for him to do like justice to New England. Not a metaphysician, and rightly discarding any claims to systematic thinking; the poet in spirit, if not always in form; the consistent idealist, yet the realist none the less, — he has illustrated the learning and thought of former times on the noblest themes, coming nearest of any to emancipating the mind of his own from the errors and dreams of past ages.

Plutarch tells us that of old they were wont to call men Φῶτα, which imports light, not only for the vehement desire man has to know, but to communicate also. And the Platonists fancied that the gods, being above men, had something whereof man did not partake, pure intellect and knowledge, and they kept on their way quietly. The beasts, being below men, had something whereof man had less, sense and growth, so they lived

quietly in their way. While man had something in him
whereof neither gods nor beasts had any trace, which
gave him all the trouble, and made all the confusion in
the world, — and that was egotism and opinion.

A finer discrimination of gifts might show that Genius ranges through this threefold dominion, partaking
in turn of their essence and degrees.

Was our poet planted so fast in intellect, so firmly
rooted in the mind, so dazzled with light, yet so cleft
withal by duplicity of gifts, that fated thus to traverse the mid-world of contrast and contrariety, he was
ever glancing forth from his coverts at life as reflected
through his dividing prism, the resident never long of
the tracts he surveyed, yet their persistent Muse nevertheless? And so housed in the Mind, and sallying
forth from thence in quest of his game, whether of persons or things, he was the Mercury, the merchantman
of ideas to his century. Nor was he personally
alone in his thinking. Beside him stood his towns-
man, whose sylvan intelligence, fast rooted in Nature,
was yet armed with a sagacity, a subtlety and strength,
that penetrated while divining the essences of creatures
and things he studied, and of which he seemed Atlas
and Head.

Forcible protestants against the materialism of their
own, as of preceding times, these masterly Idealists
substantiate beyond all question their right to the
empires they sway, — the rich estates of an original
Genius.

RECREATION.

Friday, 16.

A –FIELD all summer, all winter in-doors, was the Anglo-Saxon rule, and holds good for the Anglo-American to-day. Englishmen still, here in New England we borrow, at some variance with the sun's courses, our calendar from the old country. Ordinarily our seasons fall almost a month later, our winter hardly opening till New-year's, nor spring till All Fools' Day, the date of which can hardly fall amiss, and with All Saints' may be left indefinite in wit's almanac. Doubtless there is a closer sympathy than we suspect between souls and seasons. Sensitive to climate within as weather without, our intelligence dips or rises as the signs range from Aries to Pisces in the ideal ephemeris, measuring to faculty and member in turn the rising or falling tides, and so determining our solar and lunar periods.

> " 'T is not every day that I
> Fitted am to prophesy;
> No; but when the spirit fills
> The fantastic pinnacles
> Full of fire, then I write
> As the Godhead doth indite.
> Thus enraged, my lines are hurled,
> Like the sibyls, through the world.
> Look, how next the holy fire
> Either slakes, or doth retire;
> So the fancy carols, till when
> That brave spirit comes again."

Nature is the best dictionary and school of eloquence; genius the pupil of sun and stars, wood-lands, waters, the fields, the spectacle of things seen under all aspects, in all seasons and moods. Blot these from his vision, and the scholar's page were of small account. Letters show pale and poor from inside chambers and halls of learning alone; and whoever will deal directly with ideas, is often abroad to import the stuff of things into his diction, and clothe them in a rhetoric robust and racy, addressing the senses and mind at once. One is surprised at finding how a little exercise, though taken for the thousandth time, and along familiar haunts even, refreshes and strengthens body and mind. A turn about his grounds, a sally into the woods, climbing the hill-top, sauntering by brook-sides, brings him back with new senses and a new soul. One's handwriting becomes illuminated as he turns his leaves, the thoughts standing out distinctly, which before were blurred, and failed to show their import. Then his thought is sprightliest, and tells its tale firmly to the end. It sets flowing what blood one has in his veins, quickening wonderfully his circulations; he is valiant, humorsome, the soul prevailing in every part, and he takes hope of himself and the world around him.

An open fire, too, that best of friends to greet him within doors for most of the months; better than councils of friends to settle numerous questions wont to smoulder and fret by an air-tight, or flash forth in no lovely manner at unexpected moments. And where else is conversation possible? A countryman without an open fire will consider whether he can afford to spend himself and family to spare his wood-lot. It was comforting to see the other day on a bookseller's counter, tiles of porcelain, with suggestive devices of the graceful hospitalities of the olden time, when every mantelpiece had its attractions of fable and verse, the conversation enhanced by the friendly blaze, around which the family gathered and paid their devotions to friendships, human and divine.

> " Go where I will, thou lucky Lar, stay here
>   Close by the glittering chimney all the year."

Then, a country-seat for summer and a city residence for the winter were desirable. For recreation, the due allowance taken from business, leisures as profitable as labors, alike enjoyable, and promoting the relish for more.

> " Books, studies, business, entertain the light,
>   And sleep as undisturbed as death the night.
>   Acquaintance one would have, but when it depends
>   Not on the number, but the choice of friends.
>   His house a cottage more
>   Than palace, and should fitting be
>   For all his use, no luxury."

One's house should be roomy enough for his thought, for his family and guests; honor the ceilings, and geniality the hearthstone. Ample apartments, a charming landscape and surroundings; these have their influence on the dispositions, the tastes, manners of the inmates, and are not to be left out of account. Yet, without nobility to grace them, what were the costly palace, its parlors and parks, luxuries and elegancies, within or without, — the handsome house owing its chief beauty to the occupants, the company, one's virtues and accomplishments draw inside of the mansion ; persons being the figures that grace the edifice, else unfurnished, and but a showy pile of ostentation and folly, as desolate within as pretentious without.

> " Two things money cannot buy,
> Breeding and integrity."

" It happens," says Plutarch, " that neither rich furniture, nor moveables, nor abundance of gold, nor descent from an illustrious family, nor greatness of authority, nor eloquence, and all the charms of speaking, can procure so great a serenity of life, as a mind free from guilt and kept untainted, not only from actions but from purposes that are wicked. By this means the soul will be not only unpolluted, but not disturbed ; the fountain will run clear and unsullied, and the streams that flow from it will be just and honest deeds, full of satisfaction, a brisk energy of spirit which makes a man an enthusiast in his joy, and a tenacious memory sweeter than hope, which, as Pindar says, ' with a virgin warmth cherishes old men.' For as shrubs which are cut down with morning dew upon them, do for a long time after retain their fragrance, so the good actions of a wise man perfume his mind and leave a rich scent behind them. So that joy is, as it were, watered with those essences, and owes its flourishing to them."

GENEALOGIES.

MONDAY, 19.

ONE values his chosen place of residence, whether he be a native or not, less for its natural history and advantages than for its civil and social privileges.

> " The hills were reared, the rivers scooped in vain,
> If learning's altars vanish from the plain."

And all the more, if, while retaining the ancient manners, it cherish the family sentiment against the straggling habits which separate members so widely in our times that intercourse is had seldomer than of old ; names of kindred hardly surviving save in the fresh recollections of childhood by the dwellers apart ; far more of life than we know being planted fast in ancestral homes, the best of it associated with these, as if there were a geography of the affections that nothing could uproot.

A people can hardly have attained to nationality till it knows its ancestry and is not ashamed of its antecedents. If such studies were once deemed beneath the dignity of an American, they are no longer. We are not the less national for honoring our forefathers.

Blood is a history. Blood is a destiny. How persistent it is, let the institutions of England, Old and New, bear testimony, since on this prerogative — call it race, rank, family, nature, culture, nationality, what you will — both peoples stand and pride themselves, lion and eagle, an impregnable Saxondom, a common speech, blazoning their descent.

> " Ours is the tongue the bards sang in of old,
>   And Druids their dark knowledge did unfold ;
>   Merlin in this his prophesies did vent,
>   Which through the world of fame bear such extent.
>   Thus spake the son of Mars, and Britain bold,
>   Who first 'mongst Christian worthies is enrolled ;
>   And many thousand more, whom but to name
>   Were but to syllable great Shakespeare's fame."

A strong race, the blood flows boldly in its veins, truculent, if need be, aggressive, and holding its own, as pronounced in the women as in the men, here in New England as in Old, the dragon couchant and ready to spring in defence of privileges and titles ; magnanimous none the less, and merciful, as in the times of St. George and Bonduca. One needs but read Tacitus on the Manners of the Ancient Germans, to find the parentage of traits which still constitute the Englishmen, Old and New, showing how persistent, under every variety of geographical and political conditions, is the genius of races.

'T is due to every name that some one or more inheriting it should search out its traits and titles, as

these descend along the stream of generations and re-
appear in individuals. And we best study the fortunes
of families, of races and peoples, here at their sources.
Even heraldries have their significance. And it is ac-
counted the rule that names are entitled to the better
qualities of their emblazonries, each having something
admirable and to be honored in its origin.*

Thus the Cock is alike the herald of the dawn and
sentinel of the night; the emblem of watchfulness and of

---

* Verstegan, in his Restitution of Decayed Intelligence, in Antiquities concerning the most Noble and Renowned English Nation, 1634, treating of the
origin of names, says: —

"For a general rule, the reader may please to note, that our surnames of
families, be they of one or more syllables, that have either a *k* or a *w*, are all
of them of the ancient English race, so that neither the *k* or *w* are used in
Latin, nor in any of the three languages thereon depending, which sometimes causes confusion in the writing our names (originally coming from the
Teutonic) in Latin, Italian, French, and Spanish languages. Neither the
k nor *w* being in the Latin nor in the French, they could not be with the
Normans in use, whose language was French, as also their surnames. As
for the surnames in our Norman catalogue which have in them the letters *k*
and *w*, which the French do not use, these are not to be thought to have been
Norman, but of those gentlemen of Flanders which Baldwin, the Earl of
that country and father-in-law unto the Conqueror, did send to aid him.
Besides these, sundry other surnames do appear to have been in the Netherlands and not in Normandy; albeit they are without doubt set in the list of
the Normans. And whereas in searching for such as may remain in England of the race of the Danes, they are not such as, according to the vulgar
opinion, have their surnames ending in *son*. In the Netherlands, it is often
found that very many surnames end in *son*, as Johnson, Williamson,
Phillipson, and the like; *i. e.* sons of that name of John, etc.

Then some have their surnames according to the color of hair or complexion, as white, black, brown, gray, and reddish; and those in whom these
names from such causes begin, do thereby lose their former denomination.
Some again for their surnames have the names of beasts; and it should seem

wisdom ; of vigilance and of perseverance, and *Semper Vigilans*, the appropriate motto of family arms bearing the name with its variations.

So the poet

OF THE COCK.

"Father of Lights! what sunny seed,
　What glance of day, hast thou confined
　Unto this bird?　To all the breed
　This busy ray thou hast assigned;
　Their magnetism works all night
　And dreams of paradise and light,
　It seems their candle howe'er done
　Was tin'd and lighted at the sun."

---

for one thing or another wherein they represented some property of theirs; as lion, wolf, fox, bull, buck, hare, hart, lamb, and the like.　Others of birds; as cock, peacock, swan, crane, heron, partridge, dove, sparrow, and the like.　Others of fish; as salmon, herring, rock, pilchard, and the like. And albeit the ancestors of the bearers of these had in other times other surnames, yet because almost all these and other like names do belong to our English tongue, I do think him to be of the ancient English, and if not all, yet the most part.　And here by occasion of these names, I must note, and that as it were for a general rule, *that what family soever has their first and chief coat of arms correspondent unto their surname, it is evident sign that it had that surname before it had those arms.*"

SCHOLARSHIP.

WEDNESDAY, 28.

Apart they sit, the better know,
Why towns and talk sway men below.

FREEDOM from affairs, and leisure to entertain his thoughts, is the scholar's paradise. Hardly less the delight in comparing notes with another in conversation. It is the chiefest of satisfactions this last, where sympathy is possible and perfect. One does not see his thought distinctly till it is reflected in the image of another's. Personal perspective gives the distance necessary to bring out its significance. "There are some," says Thoreau, "whose ears help me so much that my things have a rare significance when I read to them. It is almost too good a hearing, so that, for the time, I regard my writing from too favorable a point of view." Yet the criticism of admiration is far more acceptable and the more likely to be just than that of censure. Much learning does not make an accomplished critic; taste, sensibility, sympathy, ideality, are indispensable. A man of talent may apprehend and judge fairly of works of his class. But genius alone comprehends and appreciates truly the works of genius.

Nor are all moods equally favorable for criticism. "It may be owing to my mood at the time," says

3

Goethe, " but it seems to me, that as well in treating of writings as of actions, unless one speak with a loving sympathy, a certain enthusiasm, the result is so defective as to have little value. Pleasure, delight, sympathy in things, is all that is real; and that reproduces reality in us; all else is empty and vain." One must seize the traits as they rise with the tender touch, else they elude and dissolve in the moment; pass into the obscurity out of which they emerged, and are lost forever. Much depends upon this, that one make the most of his time, and miss no propitious moods.

Rarely does one win a success with either tongue or pen. Of the books printed, scarcely never the volume entire justifies its appearance in type. Much is void of deep and permanent significance, touches nothing in one's experience, and fails to command attention. Even subjects of gravest quality, unless treated suggestively, find no place in a permanent literature. It is not enough that the thing is literally defined, stated logically; it needs to be complemented ideally, — set forth in lucid imagery to tell the story to the end. Style carries weight oftentimes when seemingly light itself. Movement is necessary, while the logic is unapparent, — all the more profound and edifying as it appeals to and speaks from the deeper instincts, and so makes claims upon the reader's mind. That is good which stands strong in its own strength, detached from local relations. So a book of thoughts suggests thought, edifies, inspires. Whatever interests at successive readings has life in it, and deserves type and paper.

My code of composition stands thus, and this is my advice to whom it may concern : —

Burn every scrap that stands not the test of all moods of criticism. Such lack longevity. What is left gains immensely. Such is the law. Very little of what is thought admirable at the writing holds good over night. Sleep on your writing ; take a walk over it ; scrutinize it of a morning ; review it of an afternoon ; digest it after a meal ; let it sleep in your drawer a twelvemonth ; never venture a whisper about it to your friend, if he be an author especially. You may read selections to sensible women, — if young the better ; and if it stand these trials, you may offer it to a publisher, and think yourself fortunate if he refuse to print it. Then you may be sure you have written a book worthy of type, and wait with assurance for a publisher and reader thirty years hence, — that is, when you are engaged in authorship that needs neither type nor publisher.

"Learning," says Fuller, "hath gained most by those books by which the printers have lost." It must be an enlightened public that asks for works the most enlightened publishers decline printing. A magazine were ruined already if it reflected its fears only. Yet one cannot expect the trade to venture reputation or money in spreading unpopular views.

Ben Jonson wrote to his bookseller : —

> " Thou that mak'st gain thy end, and wisely well
> Call'st a book good or bad, as it doth sell,
> Use mine so too ; I give thee leave, but crave
> For the luck's sake, it thus much favor have ; —
> To lie upon thy. stall, till it be sought,
> Not offered as it made suit to be bought ;
> Nor have my title page on posts or walls,
> Or in cleft-sticks advanced to make calls
> For termers, or some clerk-like serving man
> Who scarce can spell the hard names, whose knight
> 　　less can.
> If, without these vile arts it will not sell,
> Send it to Bucklersbury, there 't will, well."

Time is the best critic, and the better for his intolerance of any inferiority. And fortunate for literature that he is thus choice and exacting. Books, like character, are works of time, and must run the gauntlet of criticism to gain enduring celebrity. The best books may sometimes wait for their half century, or longer, for appreciative readers — create their readers ; the few ready to appreciate these at their issue being the most enlightened of their time, and they diffuse the light to their circle of readers. The torch of truth thus transmitted sheds its light over hemispheres, — the globe at last.

> " Hail ! native language, that with sinews weak
> Didst move my first endeavoring tongue to speak,
> And mad'st imperfect words with childish trips
> Half unpronounced slide through my infant lips,

Driving dull silence from the portal door
Where he had mutely sat two years before —
Here I salute thee, and thy pardon ask
That now I use thee in my latter task.
Now haste thee strait to do me once a pleasure,
And from thy wardrobe bring thy chiefest treasure,
Not those new-fangled toys, and trimming slight,
Which takes our late fantastics with delight,
But cull those richest robes, and gay'st attire,
Which deepest spirits and choicest wits admire."

Thus wrote Milton at the age of nineteen, and made his college illustrious and the language afterwards. Yet the purest English is not always spoken or written by graduates of universities. Speech is the fruit of breeding and of character, and one shall find sometimes in remote rural districts the language spoken in its simplicity and purity, especially by sprightly boys and girls who have not been vexed with their grammars and school tasks. Ours is one of the richest of the spoken tongues; it may not be the simplest in structure and ease of attainment; yet this last may be facilitated by simple and natural methods of studying it. Taught by masters like Ascham or Milton, students might acquire the art of speaking and of writing the language in its purity and elegance, as did these great masters in their day. Ascham lays down this sensible rule : " He that will write well in any tongue, must follow this advice of Aristotle : ' *to speak as the common people do, to think as wise men do, and so should every man understand him, and the judgment of wise men about him.*' "

George Chapman, the translator of Homer, thus speaks of the scholarly pedantries of his time, of which ours affords too many examples : —

> "For as great clerks can use no English words,
>   Because (alas! great clerks) English affords,
>   Say they, no height nor copy, — a rude tongue,
>   Since 't is their native, — but, in Greek and Latin
>   Their wits are rare, for thence true poesy sprung,
>   Through which, truth knows, they have but skill to
>   chat in,
>   Compared with what they might have in their own."

Camden said, " that though our tongue may not be as sacred as the Hebrew, nor as learned as the Greek, yet it is as fluent as the Latin, as courteous as the Spanish, as court-like as the French, and as amorous as the Italian ; so that being beautified and enriched out of these tongues, partly by enfranchising and endenizing foreign words, partly by implanting new ones with artful composition, our tongue is as copious, pithy, and significative as any in Europe."

If one would learn its riches at sight, let him glance along the pages of Richardson's Dictionary ; and at the same time survey its history from Gower and Chaucer down to our time.

" If there be, what I believe there is," says Dr. Johnson, " in every nation, a style which never becomes obsolete, a certain mode of phraseology so component and congenial to the analogy and principles of its respective language as to remain settled and unaltered ;

this style is probably to be sought in the common
intercourse of life, among those who speak only to be
understood, without ambition of eloquence. The polite are always catching modish expressions, and the
learned depart from established forms of speech, in
hope of finding or making it better ; those who wish for
distinction forsake the vulgar when the vulgar is right ;
but there is a conversation above grossness and below
refinement, where propriety resides, and where Shakespeare seems to have gathered his comic dialogues.
He is therefore more agreeable to the ears of the present age than any other author equally remote, and
among his other excellences deserves to be studied as
one of the original masters of the language."

MAY.

"Sweet country life, to such unknown
 Whose lives are others, not their own,
 But serving courts and cities, be
 Less happy, less enjoying thee."

       — Herrick.

RURAL AFFAIRS.

FAIR spring days, the farmers beginning the planting of the season's crops. One cannot well forego
the pleasures which the culture of a garden affords. He
must have a little spot upon which to bestow his affections, and own his affinities with earth and sky. The
profits in a pecuniary way may be inconsiderable, but
the pleasures are rewarding. Formerly I allowed neither hoe, spade, nor rake, not handled by myself, to
approach my plants. But when one has put his garden
within covers, to be handled in a book, he fancies he
has earned the privilege of delegating the tillage there-
after, in part, to other hands, and may please himself
with its superintendence; especially when he is so fortunate as to secure the services of any who can take
their orders without debate, and execute them with dis-
patch; and if he care to compare opinions with them,
find they have views of their own, and respect for his.
And the more agreeable if they have a pleasant humor
and the piety of lively spirits.

> " In laborer's ballads oft more piety
> God finds than in *Te Deum's* melody."

" When our ancestors," says Cato, " praised a good man, they called him a good agriculturist and a good husbandman ; he was thought to be greatly honored who was thus praised."

Without his plot of ground for tillage and ornamentation, a countryman seems out of place, its culture and keeping being the best occupation for keeping himself wholesome and sweet. The garden is the tie uniting man and nature. How civic an orchard shows in a clearing,— a garden in a prairie, as if nature waited for man to arrive and complete her, by converting the wild into the human, and thus to marry beauty and utility on the spot ! A house, too, without garden or orchard, is unfurnished, incomplete, does not fulfil our ideas of the homestead, but stands isolate, defiant in its individualism, with a savage, slovenly air, and distance, that lacks softening and blending with the surrounding landscape. Besides, it were tantalizing to note the natural advantages of one's grounds, and at the same time be unskilful to complete what nature has sketched for the hand of art to adorn and idealize. With a little skill, good taste, and small outlay of time and pains, one may render any spot a pretty paradise of beauty and comfort, — if these are not one in due combination, and not for himself only, but for those who shall inherit when he shall have left it. The rightful ownership in the landscape is born of one's genius, partakes of his essence thus wrought with the substance of the soil, the structures which he erects thereon. Whoever enriches and adorns the smallest spot, lives not in vain. For him the poet sings, the moralist points his choicest periods.

I know of nothing better suited to inspire a taste for rural affairs than a Gardener's Almanac, containing matters good to be known by country people. All the more attractive the volume if tastefully illustrated, and contain reprints of select pastoral verses, biographies, with portraits of those who have written on country affairs, and lists of their works. The old herbals, too, with all their absurdities, are still tempting books, and contain much information important for the countryman to possess.*

Cowley and Evelyn are of rural authors the most at-

---

* To the list of ancient authors, as Cato, Columella, Varro, Palladius, Virgil, Theocritus, Tibullus, selections might be added from Cowley, Marlowe, Browne, Spenser, Tusser, Dyer, Phillips, Shenstone, Cowper, Thomson, and others less known. Evelyn's works are of great value, his Kalendarium Hortense particularly. And for showing the state of agriculture and of the language in his time, Tusser's Five Hundred Points of Husbandry is full of information, while his quaint humor adds to his rugged rhymes a primitive charm. Then of the old herbals, Gerard's is best known. He was the father of English herbalists, and had a garden attached to his house in Holbern. Coles published his Adam in Eden, the Paradise of Plants, in 1659; Austin his Treatise on Fruit Trees ten years earlier. Dr. Holland's translation of the School of Salerne, or the Regiment of Health, appeared in 1649. Thos. Tryon wrote on the virtues of plants, and on health, about the same time, and his works are very suggestive and valuable. Miller, gardener to the Chelsea Gardens, gave the first edition of his Gardener's Dictionary to the press in 1731. Sir William Temple also wrote sensibly on herbs. Cowley's Six Books of Plants was published in English in 1708. Phillips' History of Cultivated Plants, etc., published in 1822, is a book of great merit. So is Culpepper's Herbal.

tractive. Cowley's Essays are delightful reading. Nor
shall I forgive his biographer for destroying the letters
of a man of whom King Charles said at his interment
in Westminster Abbey, " Mr. Cowley has not left a
better in England." The friend and correspondent of
the most distinguished poets, statesmen, and gentlemen
of his time, himself the first poet of his day, his letters
must have been most interesting and important, and
but for the unsettled temper of affairs, would doubtless
have been added to our polite literature.

Had King Charles remembered Cowley's friend Evelyn,
the compliment both to the living and dead would
have been just. Evelyn was the best of citizens and most
loyal of subjects. A complete list of his writings
shows to what excellent uses he gave himself. The
planter of forests in his time, he might be profitably con-
sulted as regards the replanting of New England now.

Respecting his planting, and the origin of his
Sylva, he writes to his friend, Lady Sunderland, August, 1690 : —

" As to the Kalendar your ladyship mentions, whatever assistance it may be to some novice gardener, sure
I am his lordship will find nothing in it worth his notice, but an old inclination to an innocent diversion ;
and the acceptance it found with my dear, and while he
lived, worthy friend, Mr. Cowley ; upon whose reputation only it has survived seven impressions, and is now
entering on the eighth, with some considerable improvement more agreeable to the present curiosity. 'T is

now, Madam, almost forty years since I first writ it, when horticulture was not much advanced in England, and near thirty years since it was published, which consideration will, I hope, excuse its many defects. If in the meantime it deserve the name of no unuseful trifle, 't is all it is capable of.

" When, many years ago, I came from rambling abroad, and a great deal more since I came home than gave me much satisfaction, and, as events have proved, scarce worth one's pursuit, I cast about how I should employ the time which hangs on most young men's hands, to the best advantage; and, when books and grave studies grew tedious, and other impertinence would be pressing, by what innocent diversions I might sometimes relieve myself without compliance to recreations I took no felicity in, because they did not contribute to any improvement of mind. This set me upon planting of trees, and brought forth my Sylva, which book, infinitely beyond my expectations, is now also calling for a fourth impression, and has been the occasion of propagating many millions of useful timber trees throughout this nation, as I may justify without immodesty, from many letters of acknowledgement received from gentlemen of the first quality, and others altogether strangers to me. His late Majesty, Charles II, was sometimes graciously pleased to take notice of it to me; and that I had by that book alone incited a world of planters to repair their broken estates and woods which the greedy rebels had wasted and made such havoc of. Upon encouragement, I was once speaking to a mighty man then in despotic power to mention the great inclination I had to serve his majesty in a little office then newly vacant (the salary I think hardly £300), whose province was to inspect the timber trees in his majesty's forests, etc., and take care of their culture and improvement; but this was conferred upon another, who, I believe, had seldom been out of the smoke of London, where, though there was a great deal of timber, there were not many trees. I confess I had an inclination to the employment upon a public account as well as its being suitable to my rural genius, born as I was, at Watton, among woods.

" Soon after this, happened the direful conflagration of this city, when, taking notice of our want of books of architecture in the English tongue, I published those most useful directions of ten of the best authors on that subject, whose works were very rarely to be had, all written in French, Latin, or Italian, and so not intelligible to our mechanics. What the fruit of that labor and cost has been, (for the sculptures, which are elegant, were very chargeable,) the great improvement of our workmen and several impressions of the copy since will best testify.

" In this method I thought proper to begin planting trees, because they would require time for growth, and be advancing to delight and shade at least, and were, therefore, by no means to be neglected and deferred, while buildings might be raised and finished in a summer or two, if the owner pleased.

" Thus, Madam, I endeavored to do my countrymen some little service, in as natural an order as I could for the improving and adorning of their estates and dwellings, and, if possible, make them in love with those useful and innocent pleasures, in exchange for a wasteful and ignoble sloth which I had observed so universally corrupted an ingenious education.

" To these I likewise added my little history of Chalcography, a treatise of the perfection of painting and of libraries, medals, with some other intermesses which might divert within doors as well as altogether without."

PASTORALS.

SATURDAY, 8.

> False were the muse, did she not bring
> Our village poet's offering —
> Haunts, fields, and groves, weaving his rhymes,
> Leaves verse and fame to coming times.

IS it for the reason that rural life here in New England furnishes nothing for pastoral verse, that our poets have as yet produced so little? Yet we cannot have had almost three centuries' residence on this side of the Atlantic, with old England's dialect, traditions, and customs still current in our rural districts for perspective, not to have so adorned life and landscape with poetic associations as to have neither honey nor dew for hiving in sweet and tender verse, though it should fall short of the antique or British models. Our fields and rivers, brooks and groves, the rural occupations of country-folk, have not been undeserving of being celebrated in appropriate verse. Our forefathers delighted in Revolutionary lore. We celebrate natural scenery, legends of foreign climes, historic events, but rarely indulge in touches of simple country life. And the idyls of New England await their poet, unless the following verses announce his arrival : —

NEW ENGLAND.

" My country, 't is for thee I strike the lyre;
  My country, wide as is the free wind's flight,
  I prize New England as she lights her fire
  In every Prairie's midst; and where the bright
  Enchanting stars shine pure through Southern night,
  She still is there the guardian on the tower,
  To open for the world a purer hour.

" Could they but know the wild enchanting thrill
  That in our homely houses fills the heart,
  To feel how faithfully New England's will
  Beats in each artery, and each small part
  Of this great Continent, their blood would start
  In Georgia, or where Spain once sat in state,
  Or Texas, with her lone star, desolate.
    .   .   .   .   .

" 'T is a New-England thought, to make this land
  The very home of Freedom, and the nurse

" Of each sublime emotion; she does stand
   Between the sunny South, and the dread curse
   Of God, who else should make her hearse
   Of condemnation to this Union's life, —
   She stands to heal this plague, and banish strife.

" I do not sing of this, but hymn the day
   That gilds our cheerful villages and plains,
   Our hamlets strewn at distance on the way,
   Our forests and the ancient streams' domains;
   We are a band of brothers, and our pains
   Are freely shared; no beggar in our roads,
   Content and peace within our fair abodes.

" In my small cottage on the lonely hill,
   Where like a hermit I must bide my time,
   Surrounded by a landscape lying still
   All seasons through as in the winters' prime,
   Rude and as homely as these verses chime,
   I have a satisfaction which no king
   Has often felt, if Fortune's happiest thing.

" 'T is not my fortune, which is meanly low,
   'T is not my merit that is nothing worth,
   'T is not that I have stores of thought below
   Which everywhere should build up heaven on earth;
   Nor was I highly favored in my birth;
   Few friends have I, and they are much to me,
   Yet fly above my poor society.

" But all about me live New-England men,
   Their humble houses meet my daily gaze, —
   The children of this land where Life again
   Flows like a great stream in sunshiny ways,
   This is a joy to know them, and my days

Are filled with love to meditate on them, —
These native gentlemen on Nature's hem.

" That I could take one feature of their life,
Then on my page a mellow light should shine;
Their days are holidays, with labor rife,
Labor the song of praise that sounds divine,
And better, far, than any hymn of mine;
The patient Earth sets platters for their food,
Corn, milk, and apples, and the best of good.

" See here no shining scenes for artist's eye,
This woollen frock shall make no painter's fame;
These homely tools all burnishing deny;
The beasts are slow and heavy, still or tame;
The sensual eye may think this labor lame;
'T is in the man where lies the sweetest art,
His true endeavor in his earnest part.

   .   .   .   .   .

" He meets the year confiding; no great throws,
That suddenly bring riches, does he use,
But like Thor's hammer vast, his patient blows
Vanquish his difficult tasks, he does refuse
To tread the path, nor know the way he views;
No sad complaining words he uttereth,
But draws in peace a free and easy breath.

   .   .   .   .   .

" This man takes pleasure o'er the crackling fire,
His glittering axe subdued the monarch oak,
He earned the cheerful blaze by something higher
Than pensioned blows, — he owned the tree he stroke,
And knows the value of the distant smoke
When he returns at night, his labor done,
Matched in his action with the long day's sun.

. . . . .

" I love these homely mansions, and to me
  A farmer's house seems better than a king's;
  The palace boasts its art, but liberty
  And honest pride and toil are splendid things;
  They carved this clumsy lintel, and it brings
  The man upon its front; Greece hath her art, —
  But this rude homestead shows the farmer's heart.

" I love to meet him on the frozen road,
  How manly is his eye, as clear as air; —
  He cheers his beasts without the brutal goad,
  His face is ruddy, and his features fair;
  His brave good-day sounds like an honest prayer;
  This man is in his place and feels his trust, —
  'T is not dull plodding through the heavy crust.

" And when I have him at his homely hearth,
  Within his homestead, where no ornament
  Glows on the mantel but his own true worth,
  I feel as if within an Arab's tent
  His hospitality is more than meant;
  I there am welcome, as the sunlight is,
  I must feel warm to be a friend of his.

. . . . .

" How many brave adventures with the cold,
  Built up the cumberous cellar of plain stone;
  How many summer heats the bricks did mould,
  That make the ample fireplace, and the tone
  Of twice a thousand winds sing through the zone
  Of rustic paling round the modest yard, —
  These are the verses of this simple bard.

" Who sings the praise of Woman in our clime?
  I do not boast her beauty or her grace;
  Some humble duties render her sublime,
  She the sweet nurse of this New-England race,
  The flower upon the country's sterile face,
  The mother of New England's sons, the pride
  Of every house where these good sons abide.

" There is a Roman splendor in her smile,
  A tenderness that owes its depth to toil;
  Well may she leave the soft voluptuous wile
  That forms the woman of a softer soil;
  She does pour forth herself a fragrant oil
  Upon the dark austerities of Fate,
  And make a garden else all desolate.

" From early morn to fading eve she stands,
  Labor's best offering on the shrine of worth,
  And Labor's jewels glitter on her hands,
  To make a plenty out of partial dearth,
  To animate the heaviness of earth,
  To stand and serve serenely through the pain,
  To nurse a vigorous race and ne'er complain.

" New-England women are New-England's pride,
  'T is fitting they should be so, they are free, —
  Intelligence doth all their acts decide,
  Such deeds more charming than old ancestry.
  I could not dwell beside them, and not be
  Enamored of them greatly; they are meant
  To charm the Poet, by their pure intent.

" A natural honest bearing of their lot,
  Cheerful at work, and happy when 't is done;
  They shine like stars within the humblest cot,

And speak for freedom centred all in one.
From every river's side I hear the son
Of some New-England woman answer me,
'Joy to our Mothers, who did make us free.'

" And when those wanderers turn to home again,
See the familiar village, and the street
Where they once frolicked, they are less than men
If in their eyes the tear-drops do not meet,
To feel how soon their mothers they shall greet:
Sons of New England have no dearer day,
Than once again within those arms to lay.

" These are her men and women; this the sight
That greets me daily when I pass their homes;
It is enough to love, it throws some light
Over the gloomiest hours; the fancy roams
No more to Italy or Greece; the loams
Whereon we tread are sacred by the lives
Of those who till them, and our comfort thrives.

" Here might one pass his days, content to be
The witness of those spectacles alway;
Bring if you may your treasure from the sea,
My pride is in my Townsmen, where the day
Rises so fairly on a race who lay
Their hopes on Heaven after their toil is o'er,
Upon this rude and bold New-England shore.

" Vainly ye pine woods rising on the height
Should lift your verdant boughs and cones aloft;
Vainly ye winds should surge around in might,
Or murmur o'er the meadow stanzas soft;
To me should nothing yield or lake or crost,

Had not the figures of the pleasant scene
Like trees and fields an innocent demean.

" I feel when I am here some pride elate,
Proud of your presence who do duty here,
For I am some partaker of your fate,
Your manly anthem vibrates in my ear;
Your hearts are heaving unconsumed by fear;
Your modest deeds are constantly supplied;
Your simpler truths by which you must abide.

" Therefore I love a cold and flinty realm,
I love the sky that hangs New England o'er,
And if I were embarked, and at the helm
I ran my vessel on New England's shore,
And dashed upon her crags, would live no more,
Rather than go seek those lands of graves
Where men who tread the fields are cowering slaves."

W. ELLERY CHANNING.

CONVERSATION.

MONDAY, 17.

IF one would learn the views of some of our most thoughtful New-England men and women, he will find their fullest and freshest expression in the discussions of the Radical Club. Almost every extreme of Liberalism is there represented, and its manners and methods are as various as the several members who take part in the readings and conversations. It is assumed that all subjects proposed for discussion are open to the freest consideration, and that each is entitled to have the

55555555

widest scope and hospitality allowed it. Truth is spherical, and seen differently according to the culture, temperament, and disposition of those who survey it from their individual standpoint. Of two or more sides, none can be absolutely right, and conversation fails if it find not the central truth from which all radiate. Debate is angular, conversation circular and radiant of the underlying unity. Who speaks deeply excludes all possibility of controversy. His affirmation is self-sufficient: his assumption final, absolute.

> Yes, yes, I see it must be so,
> The Yes alone resolves the No.

Thus holding himself above the arena of dispute, he gracefully settles a question by speaking so home to the core of the matter as to undermine the premise upon which an issue had been taken. For whoso speaks to the Personality drives beneath the grounds of difference, and deals face to face with principles and ideas.*

---

* " Dialectics treat of pure thought and of the method of arriving at it. A current misapprehension on the subject of dialectics here presents itself. Most people understand it to mean argument, and they believe that truths may be arrived at and held by such argument placed in due logical form. They demand the proof of an assertion, and imply something of weakness in the reasoning power in those who fail to give this. It is well to understand what proof means. Kant has shown us in his Critique of Pure Reason, that the course of all such ratiocination is a movement in a circle. One assumes in his premises what he wishes to prove, and then unfolds it as the result. The assumptions are in all cases mere sides of antinomies or opposite theses, each of which has validity and may be demonstrated against the other. Thus the debater moves round and round and presupposes one-sided premises which must be annulled before he can be in a state to perceive the

Good discourse sinks differences and seeks agreements. It avoids argument, by finding a common basis of agreement; and thus escapes controversy, by rendering it superfluous. Pertinent to the platform, debate is out of place in the parlor. Persuasion is the better weapon in this glittering game.

Nothing rarer than great conversation, nothing more difficult to prompt and guide. Like magnetism, it obeys its own hidden laws, sympathies, antipathies, is sensitive to the least breath of criticism. It requires natural tact, a familiarity with these fine laws, long experience, a temperament predisposed to fellowship, to hold high the discourse by keeping the substance of

---

truth. Argument of this kind the accomplished dialectician never engages in ; it is simply egotism when reduced to its lowest terms. The question assumed premises that were utterly inadmissible.

"The process of true proof does not proceed in the manner of argumentation; it does not assume its whole result in its premises, which are propositions of reflection, and then draw them out syllogistically. Speculative truth is never contained analytically in any one or in all of such propositions of reflection. It is rather the negative of them, and hence is transcendent in its entire procedure. It rises step by step, synthetically, through the negation of the principle assumed at the beginning, until, finally, the presupposition of all is reached. It is essentially a going from the part to the whole. Whatever is seized by the dialectic is turned on its varied sides, and careful note is made of its defects, *i. e.* what it lacks within itself to make it possible. That which it implies is added to it, as belonging to its totality, and thus onward progress is made until the entire comprehension of its various phases is attained. The ordinary analytic proof is seen to be shallow after more or less experience in it. The man of insight sees that it is a ' child's play, — a mere placing of the inevitable dogmatism a step or two back — that is all. *Real speculation proceeds synthetically beyond what it finds inadequate, until it reaches the adequate.*'"

WM. T. HARRIS.

things distinctly in view throughout the natural windings of the dialogue. Many can argue, not many converse. Real humility is rare everywhere and at all
times. If women have the larger share, and venture
less in general conversation, it may be from the less
confidence, not in themselves, but in those who have
hitherto assumed the lead, even in matters more spe-
cially concerning woman. Few men are diffident enough
to speak beautifully and well on the finest themes.

Conversation presupposes a common sympathy in the
subject, a great equality in the speakers ; absence of
egotism, a tender criticism of what is spoken. 'T is
this great equality and ingenuousness that renders this
game of questions so charming and entertaining, and
the more that it invites the indefinable complement of
sex. Only where the sexes are brought into sympathy,
is conversation possible. Where women are, men speak
best ; for the most part, below themselves, where women
are not. And the like holds presumably of companies
composed solely of women.

Good discourse wins from the bashful and discreet
what they have to speak, but would not, without this
provocation. The forbidding faces are Fates to over-
bear and blemish true fellowship. We give what
we are, not necessarily what we know ; nothing more,
nothing less, and only to our kind, those playing best
their parts who have the nimblest wits, taking out the
egotism, the nonsense ; putting wisdom, information,
in their place. Humor to dissolve, and wit to fledge

your theme, if you will rise out of commonplace; any amount of erudition, eloquence of phrase, scope of comprehension; figure and symbol sparingly but fitly. Who speaks to the eye, speaks to the whole mind.

Most people are too exclusively individual for conversing. It costs too great expenditure of magnetism to dissolve them; who cannot leave himself out of his discourse, but embarrasses all who take part in it. Egotists cannot converse, they talk to themselves only.

Conversation with plain people proves more agreeable and profitable, usually, than with companies more pretentious and critical. It is wont to run the deeper and stronger without impertinent interruptions, inevitable where cultivated egotism and self-assurance are present with such. There remains this resource, of ignoring civilly the interruption, and proceeding as if the intrusion had not been interposed.

> " Oft when the wise
> Appears not wise, he works the greater good."

"Never allow yourself," said Goethe, " to be betrayed into a dispute. Wise men fall into ignorance if they dispute with ignorant men." Persuasion is the finest artillery. It is the unseen guns that do execution without smoke or tumult. If one cannot win by force of wit, without cannonade of abuse, flourish of trumpet, he is out of place in parlors, ventures where he can neither forward nor grace fellowship. The great themes

are feminine, and to be dealt with delicately. Debate
is masculine ; conversation is feminine.

Here is a piece of excellent counsel from Plotinus : —
" And this may everywhere be considered, that he
who pursues our form of philosophy, will, besides all
other graces, genuinely exhibit simple and venerable
manners, in conjunction with the possession of wisdom,
and will endeavor not to become insolent or proud,
but will possess confidence, accompanied with reason,
with sincerity and candor, and great circumspection."

MARGARET FULLER.

THURSDAY, 20.

HORACE GREELEY has just issued from the
" Tribune " office a uniform edition of Margaret
Fuller's works, together with her Memoirs first published
twenty years ago. And now, while woman is the theme
of public discussion, her character and writings may be
studied to advantage. The sex has had no abler advocate. Her book entitled " Woman in the Nineteenth
Century " anticipated most of the questions now in the
air, and the leaders in the movement for woman's welfare might take its counsels as the text for their action.
Her methods, too, suggest the better modes of influence.
That she wrote books is the least of her merits. She
was greatest when she dropped her pen. She spoke
best what others essayed to say, and what women

speak best. Hers was a glancing logic that leaped straight to the sure conclusion ; a sibylline intelligence that divined oracularly ; knew by anticipation ; in the presence always, the open vision. Alas, that so much should have been lost to us, and this at the moment when it seemed we most needed and could profit by it ! Was it some omen of that catastrophe which gave her voice at times the tones of a sadness almost preternatural ? What figure were she now here in times and triumphs like ours ! She seemed to have divined the significance of woman, dared where her sex had hesitated hitherto, was gifted to untie social knots which the genius of a Plato even failed to disentangle. " Either sex alone," he said, " was but half itself." Yet he did not complement the two in honorable marriage in his social polity. " If a house be rooted in wrong," says Euripides, " it will blossom in vice." As the oak is cradled in the acorn's cup, so the state in the family. Domestic licentiousness saps every institution, the morals of the community at large, — a statement trite enough, but till it is no longer needful to be made is the commonwealth established on immovable foundations.

"Revere no God whom men adore by night."

Let the sexes be held to like purity of morals, and equal justice meted to them for any infraction of the laws of social order. Women are the natural leaders of society in whatever concerns private morals, lead where it were safe for men to follow. About the like

number as of men, doubtless, possess gifts to serve the
community at large; while most women, as most men,
will remain private citizens, fulfilling private duties.
Her vote as such will tell for personal purity, for honor,
temperance, justice, mercy, peace, — the domestic virtues upon which communities are founded, and in which
they must be firmly rooted to prosper and endure. The
unfallen souls are feminine..

Crashaw's Ideal Woman should win the love and
admiration of her sex as well as ours.

> " Whoe'er she be
>   That not impossible she
>   That shall command my heart and me;

> " Where'er she lie
>   Lock'd up from mortal eye
>   In shady leaves of destiny;

> " Till that ripe birth
>   Of studied fate stand forth,
>   And teach her fair steps to our earth :

> " Till that divine
>   Idea take a shrine
>   Of crystal flesh, through which to shine,

> " Meet you her my wishes,
>   Bespeak her to my blisses,
>   And be ye called my absent kisses.

" I wish her beauty
    That owes not all its duty
    To gaudy tire, or glistening shoe-ty.

" Something more than
    Taffata or tissue can,
    Or rampant feather, or rich fan.

" More than the spoil
    Of shop, or silkworm's toil,
    Or a bought blush, or a set smile.

" A face that's best
    By its own beauty drest,
    And can alone command the rest.

" A face made up
    Out of no other shop
    Than what nature's white hand sets ope.

" A cheek where youth
    And blood, with pen of truth,
    Write what the reader sweetly rueth.

" A cheek where grows
    More than a morning rose,
    Which to no box his being owes.

" Lips, where all day
    A lover's kiss may play,
    Yet carry nothing thence away.

" Looks, that oppress
    Their richest tires, but dress
    And clothe their simplest nakedness.

" Eyes, that displaces
  The neighbor diamond and out-faces
  That sunshine by their own sweet graces.

" Tresses, that wear
  Jewels, but to declare
  How much themselves more precious are.

" Whose native ray
  Can tame the wanton day
  Of gems that in their bright shades play.

" Each ruby there,
  Or pearl that dare appear,
  Be its own blush, be its own tear.

" A well-tamed heart,
  For whose more noble smart
  Love may be long choosing a dart.

" Eyes, that bestow
  Full quivers on Love's bow,
  Yet pay less arrows than they owe.

" Smiles, that can warm
  The blood, yet teach a charm
  That chastity shall take no harm.

" Blushes, that been
  The burnish of no sin,
  Nor flames of aught too hot within.

" Days, that need borrow
  No part of their good morrow
  From a fore-spent night of sorrow.

6

" Days, that in spite
  Of darkness, by the light
  Of a clear mind are day all night.

" Life, that dares send
  A challenge to his end,
  And when it comes say, ' Welcome, friend.'

" Sydneian showers
  Of sweet discourse, whose powers
  Can crown old Winter's head with flowers.

" Soft silken hours,
  Open suns, shady bowers,
  'Bove all, nothing within that lowers.

" Whate'er delight
  Can make day's forehead bright,
  Or give down to the wings of night.

" In her whole frame,
  Have nature all the name,
  Art and ornament the shame.

" Her flattery,
  Picture and poesy,
  Her counsel her own virtue be.

" I wish her store
  Of worth may leave her poor
  Of wishes ; and I wish — no more."

CHILDHOOD.

MY little grandsons visit me at this becoming season of birds and apple blossoms. They accompany me to the brook, and are pleased with their willow whistles and sail-boats, — toys delightful to childhood from the first. Their manners, that first of accomplishments, delight us in return, showing that the sense of beauty has dawned and their culture fairly begun. 'T is a culture to watch them through their days' doings. Endless their fancies and engagements. What arts, accomplishments, graces, are woven in their playful panorama; the scene shifting with the mood, and all in keeping with the laws of thought and of things. Verily, there are invisible players playing their parts through these pretty puppets all day long.

To conceive a child's acquirements as originating in nature, dating from his birth into his body, seems an atheism that only a shallow metaphysical theology could entertain in a time of such marvellous natural knowledge as ours. " I shall never persuade myself," said Synesius, " to believe my soul to be of like age with my body." And yet we are wont to date our birth, as that of the babes we christen, from the body's advent, so duteously inscribed in our family registers, as if time and space could chronicle the periods of the immortal mind, and mark its longevity by our chronometers.* Only a God could inspire a child with the intimations seen in its first pulse-plays; the sprightly attainments of a single day's doings afford the liveliest proofs of an omniscient Deity revealing his attributes in the motions of the little one! Nor is maternity less a special inspiration throbbing ceaselessly with childhood as a protecting Providence, lifelong. Comes not the mother to make the Creator's word sure that all he has made is verily good? For without mother and wife, what more than a rough outline of divinity were drawn? "That man," says Euripides, "hath made his fortune who hath married a good wife." For what would some of us have accomplished, what should we have not done, misdone, without her counsels to temper our adventurous idealism? Heaven added a new power to creation when it sent woman into it to complete what He had designed.

> "He is a parricide to his mother's name,
>   And with an impious hand, murthers her fame,
>   Who wrongs the praise of woman; that dares write
>   Libels on saints, or with foul ink requite
>   The milk they lent us."

---

* "Infants," says Olympiodorus, "are not seen to laugh for some time after birth, but pass the greater part of their time in sleep; however, in their sleep they appear both to smile and cry. But can this any otherwise happen than through the soul agitating the circulations of their animal nature in conformity with the passions it has experienced before birth into the body? Besides, our looking into ourselves when we seek to discover any truth, shows that we inwardly contain truth, though concealed in the darkness of oblivion." Does atom animate and revive thought, or thought animate and illuminate atom? And which the elder?

When one becomes indifferent to women, to children and young people, he may know that he is superannuated, and has withdrawn from whatsoever is sweetest and purest in human existence. One of the happiest rewards of age is the enjoyment of children. And when these inherit one's better gifts and graces, sinking the worse, or omitting them altogether, what can be added to fill the cup of parental gratitude and delight? I fail to comprehend how the old and young folks are to enjoy a future heaven together, unless they have learned to partake in the enjoyments of this. Shall we picture future separate heavens for them?

Sing, sing, the immortals,
    The ancients of days,
Ever crowding the portals
    Of earth's populous ways;

The babes ever stealing
Into Eden's glad feeling;
The fore-world revealing
God's face, ne'er concealing.

Sing, sing, the child's fancies,
Its graces and glances,
Plans, pastimes, surprises,
Slips, sorrows, surmises.

Youth's trials and treasures,
Its hopes without measures,

Its labors and leisures;
His world all before him,
High heaven all o'er him;
Life's lengthening story,
Opening glory on glory;
By age ne'er o'ertaken,
By youth near forsaken.

Sings none this fair story,
But dwellers in its glory;
Who would the youth see,
A youth he must be;
Heaven's kingdom alone
To children doth come.

The family is the sensitive plant of civility, the measure of culture. Take the census of the homes, and you have the sum total of character and civilization in any community. Sown in the family, the seeds of holiness are here to be cherished and ripened for immortality. Here is the seminary of the virtues, the graces, accomplishments, that adorn and idealize existence. From this college we graduate for better or for worse. This faculty of the affections, this drinking freshly at the springs of genius and sensibility, this intimacy with the loveliest and best in life, is the real schooling, the truest discipline, without which neither mind nor heart flourish; all other advantages being of secondary account; wealth, wit, beauty, social position, books, travel, fellowships, are but sounding names, opportunities of inferior importance, compared with this endowment of personal influences.

Here, in this atmosphere of love and sympathy, character thrives and ripens. And were the skill for touching its tender sensibilities, calling forth its budding gifts, equal to the charms the child has for us, what noble characters would graduate from our families, — the community receiving its members accomplished in the Personal graces, the state its patriots, the church its saints, all glorifying the race. One day the highest culture of the choicest gifts will be deemed essential to the heads of families, and the arts of nurture and of culture honored as the art of arts.

"Boys are dear to divinity," dear to all mankind. What more charming than to watch the dawning intelligence, clearing itself from the mists which obscure its vision of the world into which it has but lately entered? The more attractive, since a fine sentiment then mingles mythically with the freshness of thought, confuses the sexes, as if the boy were being transformed into the girl, first entering her wider world of affection; and the girl in turn were being metamorphosed into the boy, first becoming conscious of the newer world of intellect; each entering, by instinct, into the mind of the other. I know not which is the more charming each in their ways, the coy manners of girls, or the shy behavior of beautiful boys, — mysteries both to each other, nor less to their elders. 'T is the youthful sentiment, whether feminine or masculine, that renders friendship delight-

ful, the world lovely; this gone, all is gone that life
can enjoy. "There are periods in one's life," says
Pythagoras, "which it is not in the power of any casual
person to connect finely, these being expelled by one
another, unless some sympathetic friend conduct him
from birth in a beautiful and upright manner."

PYTHAGORAS.

Of the great educators of antiquity, I esteem Pythagoras the most eminent and successful. Everything of his doctrine and discipline comes commended
by its elegance and humanity, and justifies the name he
bore of the golden-souled Samian, and founder of the
Greek culture. He seems to have stood in providential
nearness to the human sensibility, as if his were a ma-
ternal relation as well, and he owned the minds whom
he nurtured and educated. The first of philosophers,
taking the name for its modesty of pretension, he
justified his claim to it in the attainments and services
of his followers; his school having given us Socrates,
Plato, Pericles, Plutarch, Plotinus, and others of almost
equal fame, founders of states and cultures.

He was most fortunate in his biographer. For, next
to the Gospels, I know of nothing finer of the kind
than the mythological portrait drawn of him by Jambli-
chus, his admiring disciple, and a philosopher worthy
of his master. How mellow the coloring, the drapery
disposed so gracefully about the person he paints! I

look upon this piece of nature with ever fresh delight, so reverend, humane, so friendly in aspect and Olympian. Nor is the interest less, but enhanced rather by the interfusion of fable into the personal history, the charm of a subtle idealism being thus given it, relating him thereby to the sacred names of all times. There is in him an Oriental splendor, as of sunrise, reflected on statues, blooming in orchards, an ambrosial beauty and sweetness, as of autumnal fruits and of women.

> " In all he did,
> Some picture of the golden times was hid."

Personally, he is said to have been the most beautiful and godlike of all those who had been celebrated in history before his time. As a youth, his aspect was venerable and his habits strictly temperate, so that he was reverenced and honored by elderly men. He attracted the attention of all who saw him, and appeared admirable in all eyes. He was adorned by piety and discipline, by a mode of life transcendently good, by firmness of soul, and by a body in due subjection to the mandates of reason. In all his words and actions, he discovered an inimitable quiet and serenity, not being subdued at any time by anger, emulation, contention, or any precipitation of conduct. He was reverenced by the multitude as one under the influence of divine inspiration. He abstained from all intoxicating drinks, and from animal food, confining himself to a chaste nutriment. Hence, his sleep was short and undisturbed, his soul vigilant and pure, his body in a state of perfect and invariable health. He was free from the superstitions of his time, and pervaded with a deep sense of duty towards God, and veneration for his divine attributes and immanency in things. He fixed his mind so intently on the attainment of wisdom, that systems and mysteries inaccessible to others were opened to him by his magic genius and sincerity of purpose. The great principle with which he started, that of being a seeker rather than possessor of truth, seemed ever to urge him forward with a diligence and an activity unprecedented in the history of the past, and perhaps unequalled since. He visited every man who could claim any degree of fame for wisdom or learning, whilst the relics of antiquity and the simplest operations of nature seemed to yield to his researches ; and we moderns are using his eyes in many departments of activity into which pure thought enters, being indebted to him for important discoveries alike in science and metaphysics.

" His institution at Crotona was the most comprehensive and complete of any of which we read. His aim being at once a philosophical school, a religious brotherhood, and a political association. And all these characters appear to have been inseparably united in the founder's mind. It must be considered as a proof of upright intentions in Pythagoras which ought to rescue him from all suspicion of selfish motives, that he chose for his associates persons whom he deemed capable of grasping the highest truths which he could communicate, and was not only willing to teach them all he knew, but regarded the utmost cultivation of the intellectual faculties as a necessary preparation for the work to which he destined them. He instituted a society, an order, as one may now call it, composed of young men, three hundred in number, carefully selected from the noblest families, not only of Crotona, but of the other Italian cities.

" Those who confided themselves to the guidance of his doctrine and discipline, conducted themselves in the following manner : —

" They performed their morning walks alone in places where there happened to be an appropriate solitude and quiet, and where there were temples and groves, and other things adapted to give delight. For they thought it was not proper to converse with any one till they had rendered their own soul sedate and co-harmonized with the reasoning power. For they apprehended it to be a thing of a turbulent nature to mingle in a crowd as soon as they rose from bed. But after the morning walk, they associated with each other, and employed themselves in discussing doctrines and disciplines, and in the correction of their manners and lives.

" They employed their time after dinner, which consisted of bread and honey without wine, in domestic labors and economies, and in the hospitalities due to strangers and their guests, according to the laws. All business of this sort was transacted during these hours of the day.

" When it was evening, they again betook themselves to walking, yet not singly as in the morning walk, but in parties of two or three, calling to mind, as they walked, the disciplines which they had learned, and exercising themselves in beautiful studies.

" After bathing again, they went to supper; no more than ten meeting together for this purpose. This meal they finished before the setting of the sun. It was of wine and maize, bread and salad. They were of opinion that any animal, not naturally noxious to the human race, should·neither be injured nor slain.

" After supper, libations were performed; and these were succeeded by readings, the youngest reading, and the eldest ordering what should be read and after what manner.

" They wore a white and pure garment, and slept on beds the coverlets of which were of white linen."

CONVERSATION WITH CHILDREN.

MONDAY, 24.

MY book of Conversations, held with Children in Boston near forty years ago, has found an admiring reader at last. He writes: —

" I have just found in a second-hand bookstore your two volumes of Conversations on the Gospels, and have read them with benefit and delight. Nowhere have I seen the Gospels so spiritualized, so rationalized,

Platonized. The *naïveté* aside, it seems the product of a company of idealists. Is it possible that common human nature in children, thrown upon its own resources, can exhibit such intelligence, or instinct, if you please to call it so? Were these children taken as they came, or were they selected, culled?"

They came from families occupying various social advantages, and were a fair average of children thus born and bred. I give a sample of one of the conversations as reported from their lips at the time. Their ages were from six to twelve years.

CONVERSATION ON WORSHIP.

Mr. Alcott read (having previously read the beginning) the remainder of the Conversation of Jesus with the woman of Samaria (John iv. 16–30), —

16. Jesus saith unto her, Go call thy husband, and come hither.

17. The woman answered and said, I have no husband. Jesus said unto her, Thou hast well said I have no husband:

18. For thou hast had five husbands, and he whom thou now hast is not thy husband: in that saidst thou truly.

19. The woman said unto him, Sir, I perceive that thou art a prophet.

20. Our fathers worshipped in this mountain; and ye say that in Jerusalem is the place where men ought to worship.

21. Jesus saith unto her, Woman, believe me, the hour cometh when ye shall neither in this mountain, nor yet at Jerusalem, worship the Father.

22. Ye worship ye know not what: we know what we worship, for salvation is of the Jews.

23. But the hour cometh, and now is, when the true worshippers shall worship the Father in spirit and in truth: for the father seeketh such to worship him.

24. God *is* a Spirit: and they that worship him must worship *him* in spirit and in truth.

25. The woman saith unto him, I know that Messias cometh. which is called Christ; when he is come, he will tell us all things.

26. Jesus saith unto her, I that speak unto thee am *he*.

27. And upon this came his disciples, and marvelled that he talked with the woman: yet no man said, What seekest thou? or, Why talkest thou with her?

28. The woman then left her water-pot, and went her way into the city, and saith to the men,

29. Come, see a man which told me all things that ever I did: is not this the Christ?

30. Then they went out of the city, and came unto him.

Before he had time to ask the usual question, —

SAMUEL T. (*spoke*). I was most interested in this verse: " He that drinks of this water shall thirst again, but he that drinks of the water that I shall give him, shall never thirst." He means by this, that those who heard what he taught, and did it, should live always, should never die, their spirits should never die.

MR. ALCOTT. Can spirits die?

SAMUEL T. For a spirit to die is to leave off being good.

EDWARD J. I was interested in the words, " For the water I shall give him will be in him a well of water." I think it means that when people are good and getting better, it is like water springing up always. They have more and more goodness.

Samuel R. Water is an emblem of holiness.

Mr. Alcott. Water means spirit, pure and unsoiled.

Edward J. It is holy spirit.

Ellen. I was most interested in these words : " Ye worship ye know not what." The Samaritans worship idols, and there was no meaning to that.

Mr. Alcott. What do you mean by their worshipping idols?

Ellen. They cared about things more than God.

Mr. Alcott. What kind of false worship do you think Jesus was thinking about when he said : " Woman, the hour is coming and now is, when neither in this mountain — " ?

Ellen. Oh! she thought the place of worship was more important than the worship itself.

Mr. Alcott. Well! how did Jesus answer that thought?

Ellen. He told her what she ought to worship, which was more important than where.

Mr. Alcott. Some of you, perhaps, have made this mistake, and thought that we only worshipped God in churches, and on Sundays. How is it, — who has thought so?

(*Several held up hands, smiling.*)

Who knew that we could worship God anywhere?

(*Others held up hands.*)

What other worship is there besides that in the church?

EDWARD J.   The worship in our hearts.

MR. ALCOTT.   How is that carried on?

EDWARD J.   By being good.

NATHAN.   We worship God by growing better.

AUGUSTINE.   We worship God when we repent of doing wrong.

JOSIAH.   I was most interested in this verse: " God is a spirit, and they that worship him must worship him in spirit and in truth.". It means that to feel our prayers is more important than to say the words.

LEMUEL.   And when we pray and pray sincerely.

MR. ALCOTT.   What is praying sincerely?

LEMUEL.   Praying the truth.

MR. ALCOTT.   What is to be done in praying the truth?   When you think of prayer, do you think of a position of the body — of words?

LEMUEL (*earnestly*).   I think of something else, but I cannot express it.

MR. ALCOTT.   Josiah is holding up his hand; can he express it?

JOSIAH (*burst out*).   To pray, Mr. Alcott, is to be good, really; you know it is better to be bad before people and to be good to God alone, because then we are good for goodness sake, and not to be seen, and not for people's sake.   Well, so it is about prayer.   There must be nothing outward with prayer; but we must have some words, sometimes; sometimes we need not.

If we don't feel the prayer, it is worse than never to say a word of prayer. It is wrong not to pray, but it is more wrong to speak prayer and not pray. We had better do nothing about it, Mr. Alcott! we must say words in a prayer, and we must feel the words we say, and we must do what belongs to the words.

Mr. Alcott. Oh! there must be doing, must there?

Josiah. Oh! yes, Mr. Alcott! doing is the most important part. We must ask God for help, and at the same time try to do the thing we are to be helped about. If a boy should be good all day, and have no temptation, it would not be very much; there would be no improvement; but if he had temptation, he could pray and feel the prayer, and try to overcome it, and would overcome it; and then there would be a real prayer and a real improvement. That would be something. Temptation is always necessary to a real prayer, I think. I don't believe there is ever any real prayer before there is a temptation; because we may think and feel and say our prayer; but there cannot be any doing, without there is something to be done.

Mr. Alcott. Well, Josiah, that will do now. Shall some one else speak?

Josiah. Oh, Mr. Alcott, I have not half done!

Edward J. Mr. Alcott, what is the use of responding in church?

Mr. Alcott. Cannot you tell?

Edward J. No; I never knew.

Josiah. Oh! Mr. Alcott!

5

Mr. Alcott. Well, Josiah, do you know?

Josiah. Why, Edward! is it not just like a mother's telling her child the words? The child wants to pray; it don't know how to express its real thoughts, as we often say to Mr. Alcott here; and the mother says words, and the child repeats after her the words.

Edward J. Yes; but I don't see what good it does.

Josiah. What! if the mother says the words, and the child repeats them and feels them, — really wants the things that are prayed for, — can't you see that it does some good?

Edward J. It teaches the word-prayer — it is not the real prayer.

Josiah. Yet it must be the real prayer, and the real prayer must have some words.

But, Mr. Alcott, I think it would be a great deal better, if, at church, everybody prayed for themselves. I don't see why one person should pray for all the rest. Why could not the minister pray for himself, and the people pray for themselves? and why should not all communicate their thoughts? Why should only one speak? Why should not all be preachers? Everybody could say something; at least, everybody could say their own prayers, for they know what they want. Every person knows the temptations they have, and people are tempted to do different things. Mr. Alcott, I think Sunday ought to come oftener.

Mr. Alcott. Our hearts can make all time Sunday.

Josiah. Why, then, nothing could be done! There

must be week-days, I know — some week-days ; I said, Sunday oftener.

Mr. Alcott. But you wanted the prayers to be doing prayers. Now some of the rest may tell me, how you could pray doing prayers.

George K. Place is of no consequence. I think prayer is in our hearts. Christian prayed in the cave of Giant Despair. We can pray anywhere, because we can have faith anywhere.

Mr. Alcott. Faith, then, is necessary?

George K. Yes ; for it is faith that makes the prayer.

Mr. Alcott. Suppose an instance of prayer in yourself.

George K. I can pray going to bed or getting up.

Mr. Alcott. You are thinking of time, place, words.

George K. And feelings and thoughts.

Mr. Alcott. And action?

George K. Yes ; action comes after.

John B. When we have been doing wrong and are sorry, we pray to God to take away the evil.

Mr. Alcott. What evil, the punishment?

John B. No ; we want the forgiveness.

Mr. Alcott. What is for-give-ness? Is it anything given?

Lemuel. Goodness, holiness.

John B. And the evil is taken away.

Mr. Alcott. Is there any action in all this?

John B. Why, yes ; there is thought and feeling.

Mr. Alcott. But it takes the body also to act; what do the hands do?

John B. There is no prayer in the hands.

Mr. Alcott. You have taken something that belongs to another; you pray to be forgiven; you wish not to do so again; you are sorry. Is there anything to do?

John B. If you injure anybody, and can repair it, you must, and you will, if you have prayed sincerely; but that is not the prayer.

Mr. Alcott. Would the prayer be complete without it?

John B. No.

Andrew. Prayer is in the spirit.

Mr. Alcott. Does the body help the spirit?

Andrew. It don't help the prayer.

Mr. Alcott. Don't the lips move?

Andrew. But have the lips anything to do with the prayer?

Mr. Alcott. Yes; they may. The whole nature may act together; the body pray; and I want you to tell an instance of a prayer in which are thoughts, feelings, action; which involves the whole nature, body and all. There may be prayer in the palms of our hands.

Andrew. Why, if I had hurt anybody, and was sorry and prayed to be forgiven, I suppose I should look round for some medicine and try to make it well.

(*Mr. Alcott here spoke of the connection of the mind with the body, in order to make his meaning clearer.*)

SAMUEL R. If I had a bad habit, and should ask God for help to break it; and then should try so as really to break it, that would be a prayer.

CHARLES. Suppose I saw a poor beggar boy hurt or sick, and all bleeding; and I had very nice clothes, and was afraid to soil them, or from any such cause should pass him by, and by and by I should look back and see another boy helping him, and should be really sorry and pray to be forgiven, that would be a real prayer; but if I had done the kindness at the time of it, that would have been a deeper prayer.

AUGUSTINE. When anybody has done wrong, and does not repent for a good while, but at last repents and prays to be forgiven, it may be too late to do anything about it; yet that might be a real prayer.

MR. ALCOTT. Imagine a real doing prayer in your life.

LUCIA. Suppose, as I was going home from school, some friend of mine should get angry with me, and throw a stone at me; I could pray not to be tempted to do the same, to throw a stone at her, and would not.

MR. ALCOTT. And would the not doing anything in that case be a prayer and an action? Keeping your body still would be the body's part of it.

LUCIA. Yes.

ELLEN. I heard a woman say, once, that she could pray best when she was at work; that when she was scouring the floor she would ask God to cleanse her mind.

Mr. Alcott.   I will now vary my question.   Is there any prayer in Patience?

All.   A great deal.

Mr. Alcott.   In Impatience?

All.   No; not any.

Mr. Alcott.   In Doubt?

George K.   No; but in Faith.

Mr. Alcott.   In Laziness?

All (*but Josiah*).   No; no kind of prayer.

Josiah.   I should think that Laziness was the prayer of the body, Mr. Alcott.

Mr. Alcott.   Yes; it seems so.   The body tries to be still more body; it tries to get down into the clay; it tries to sink; but the spirit is always trying to lift it up and make it do something.

Edward J.   Lazy people sometimes have passions that make them act.

Mr. Alcott.   Yes; they act downwards.   Is there any prayer in Disobedience?

All.   No.

Mr. Alcott.   Is there any in submission?   In forbearing when injured?   In suffering for a good object?   In self-sacrifice?

All (*eagerly to each question*).   Yes.   Yes.   Yes. Yes.

(*Mr. Alcott here made some very interesting remarks on loving God with all our heart, soul, mind, etc., and the Idea of Devotion it expressed.   Josiah wanted to speak constantly, but Mr. Alcott checked him, that the*

*others might have opportunity, though the latter wished
to yield to Josiah.*)

JOSIAH (*burst out*). Mr. Alcott! you know Mrs.
Barbauld says in her hymns, everything is prayer;
every action is prayer; all nature prays; the bird
prays in singing; the tree prays in growing; men pray;
men can pray more; we feel; we have more — more
than nature; we can know and do right; Conscience
prays; all our powers pray; action prays. Once we
said here, that there was a " Christ in the bottom of
our spirits" when we try to be good; then we pray in
Christ; and that is the whole.*

MR. ALCOTT. Yes, Josiah, that is the whole. That
is Universal Prayer — the adoration of the Universe to
its Author!

CHARLES. I was most interested in this verse —
" The day is coming, and now is, when men shall worship the Father," etc. I think that this means that
people are about to learn what to worship, and where.

MR. ALCOTT. Have you learned this to-day?

CHARLES. Yes; I have learnt some new things, I
believe.

MR. ALCOTT. What are you to worship?

CHARLES. Goodness.

MR. ALCOTT. Where is it?

CHARLES. Within.

---

* This improvisation is preserved in its words. Josiah, it may be named,
was under seven years of age, and the other children were chiefly between
the ages of six and twelve years.

MR. ALCOTT. Within what?

CHARLES. Conscience, or God.

MR. ALCOTT. Are you to worship Conscience?

CHARLES. Yes.

MR. ALCOTT. Is it anywhere but in yourself?

CHARLES. Yes; it is in Nature.

MR. ALCOTT. Is it in other people?

CHARLES. Yes; there is more or less of it in other people, unless they have taken it out.

MR. ALCOTT. Can it be entirely taken out?

CHARLES. Goodness always lingers in Conscience.

MR. ALCOTT. Is Conscience anywhere but in Human Nature?

CHARLES. It is in the Supernatural.

MR. ALCOTT. You said at first that there was something in outward Nature which we should worship.

CHARLES. No; I don't think we should worship anything but the Invisible.

MR. ALCOTT. What is the Invisible?

CHARLES. It is the Supernatural.

JOHN B. It is the Inward — the Spiritual. But I don't see why we should not worship the sun a little as well —

MR. ALCOTT. As well as the Sun-maker? But there are sun-worshippers.

JOHN B. Yes; a little; for the sun gives us light and heat.

MR. ALCOTT. What is the difference between your feeling when you think of the sun, or the ocean (*he described some grand scenes*), and when you think of Conscience acting in such cases as — (*he gave some striking instances of moral power*). Is there not a difference?

(*They raised their hands.*)

What is the name of the feeling with which you look at Nature?

SEVERAL. Admiration.

MR. ALCOTT. But when Conscience governs our weak body, is it not a Supernatural Force? Do you not feel the awe of the inferior before a superior nature? And is not that worship? The sun cannot produce it.

JOSIAH. Spirit worships Spirit. Clay worships Clay.

MR. ALCOTT. Wait a moment, Josiah. I wish first to talk with the others; let me ask them this question: Do you feel that Conscience is stronger than the mountain, deeper and more powerful than the ocean? Can you say to yourself, I can remove this mountain?

JOSIAH (*burst out*). Yes, Mr. Alcott! I do not mean that with my body I can lift up a mountain — with my hand; but I can feel; and I know that my Conscience is greater than the mountain, for it can feel and do; and the mountain cannot. There is the mountain, there! It was made, and that is all. But my Conscience can grow. It is the same kind of Spirit as made the mountain be, in the first place. I do not know what it may be and do. The Body is a mountain, and the Spirit says, be moved, and it is moved into another place.

Mr. Alcott, we think too much about clay. We should think of Spirit. I think we should love Spirit, not Clay. I should think a mother now would love her baby's Spirit; and suppose it should die, that is only the Spirit bursting away out of the Body. It is alive; it is perfectly happy. I really do not know why people mourn when their friends die. I should think it would be matter of rejoicing. For instance: now, if we should go out into the street and find a box — an old dusty box — and should put into it some very fine pearls, and by and by the box should grow old and break, why, we should not even think about the box; but if the pearls were safe, we should think of them and nothing else. So it is with the Soul and Body. I cannot see why people mourn for bodies.

Mr. Alcott. Yes, Josiah; that is all true, and we are glad to hear it. Shall some one else now speak besides you?

Josiah. Oh, Mr. Alcott! then I will stay in the recess and talk.

Mr. Alcott. When a little infant opens its eyes upon this world, and sees things out of itself, and has the feeling of admiration, is there in that feeling the beginning to worship?

Josiah. No, Mr. Alcott; a little baby does not worship. It opens its eyes on the outward world, and sees things, and perhaps wonders what they are; but it don't know anything about them or itself. It don't know the uses of anything; there is no worship in it.

Mr. Alcott. But in this feeling of wonder and admiration which it has, is there not the beginning of worship that will at last find its object?

Josiah. No; there is not even the beginning of worship. It must have some temptation, I think, before it can know the thing to worship.

Mr. Alcott. But is there not a feeling that comes up from within, to answer to the things that come to the eyes and ears?

Josiah. But feeling is not worship, Mr. Alcott.

Mr. Alcott. Can there be worship without feeling?

Josiah. No; but there can be feeling without worship. For instance, if I prick my hand with a pin, I feel, to be sure, but I do not worship.

Mr. Alcott. That is bodily feeling. But may not the little infant find its power to worship in the feeling which is first only admiration of what is without.

Josiah. No, no; I know what surprise is, and I know what admiration is; and perhaps the little creature feels that. But she does not know enough to know that she has conscience, or that there is temptation. My little sister feels, and she knows some things; but she does not worship.

Mr. Alcott. Now I wish you all to think. What have we been talking about to-day?

Charles. Spiritual Worship.*

---

* Here I was obliged to pause, as I was altogether fatigued with keeping my pen in long and uncommonly constant requisition. I was enabled to preserve the words better than usual, because Josiah had so much of the conversation, whose enunciation is slow, and whose fine choice of language and steadiness of mind, makes him easy to follow and remember. — *Recorder.*

PLUTARCH'S LETTER TO HIS WIFE.

S UNDAY, 30.

I SOMETIMES think the funeral rites and cemeteries of a people best characterize its piety. Contrast the modern with the primitive grave-yards, — their funeral services so dismal, doleful, despairing : as if their faith in immortality were fittest clad in sables, and death were a descent of souls, instead of an ascension. What fairer views of life and of immortality our fresher faith exhibits. Verdure, cheerful marbles, tasteful avenues, flowers, simple epitaphs, inscriptions celebrating the virtues properly humane. What in the range of English lyric verse is comparable to Wordsworth's ode, entitled Intimations of Immortality in Childhood, or his prose Essay on Epitaphs. Nor is the contrast so disparaging between these and Pagan moralities. Christianity can hardly add to the sweetness and light, the tenderness, trust in man's future well-being, shown in Plutarch's consolatory Letter to his Wife on the death of his little daughter. One becomes more Christian, even, in copying it.

PLUTARCH TO HIS WIFE — ALL HEALTH.

" As for the messenger you dispatched to tell me of the death of my little daughter, it seems he missed his way as he was going to Athens. But when I came to Tanagra I heard of it by my niece. I suppose by this time the funeral is over. I wish that whatever happens, as well now as hereafter, may create you no dissatisfaction. But if you have designedly let anything alone, depending upon my judgment, thinking better to determine the point if I were with you, I pray let it be without ceremony or timorous superstition, which I know are far from you. Only, dear wife, let you and me bear our affliction with patience. I know very well, and do comprehend what loss we have had; but if I should find you grieve beyond measure, this would trouble me more than the thing itself; for I had my birth neither from a stock nor stone, and you know it full well; I having been assistant to you in the education of so many children, which we brought up at home under our own care.

"This much-lamented daughter was born after four sons, which made me call her by your own name; therefore, I know she was dear to you, and grief must have a peculiar pungency in a mind tenderly affectionate to children, when you call to mind how naturally witty and innocent she was, void of anger, and not querulous. She was naturally mild and compassionate, to a miracle. And she showed delight in, and gave a specimen of, her humanity and gratitude towards anything that had obliged her, for she would pray her nurse to give suck, not only to other children, but to her very playthings, as it were courteously inviting them to her table, and making the best cheer for them she could. Now, my dear wife, I see no reason why these and the

like things which delighted us so much when she was
alive, should, upon remembrance of them, afflict us
when she is dead. But I also fear, lest while we cease
from sorrowing, we should forget her, as Clymene
said : —

> I hate the handy horned bow,
> And banish youthful pastimes now,

because she would not be put in mind of her son, by
the exercises he had been used to. For nature always
shuns such things as are troublesome. But since our
little daughter afforded all our senses the sweetest and
most charming pleasure, so ought we to cherish her
memory, which will in many ways conduce more to our
joy than grief. And it is but just that the same argu-
ments which we have ofttimes used to others should
prevail upon ourselves at this so seasonable a time, and
that we should not supinely sit down and overwhelm
the joys which we have tasted with a multiplicity of
new griefs. Moreover, they who were present at the
funeral, report this with admiration, that you neither
put on mourning, nor disguised yourself, or any of your
maids ; neither were there any costly preparations, nor
magnificent pomp, but that all things were managed
with prudence and moderation. And it seemed not
strange to me, that you, who never used richly to dress
yourself, for the theatre or other public solemnities,
esteeming such magnificence vain and useless, even in
matters of delight, have now practised frugality on
this finest occasion. . . . There is no philosopher of

your acquaintance who is not in love with your frugality, both in apparel and diet; nor a citizen, to
whom the simplicity and plainness of your dress is
not conspicuous, both at religious sacrifices and public shows in the theatre. Formerly, also, you discovered on a like occasion, a great constancy of mind when
you lost your eldest son. And again, when the lovely
Charon left us. For I remember when the news was
brought me of my son's death, as I was returning home
with some friends and guests who accompanied me to
my house, that when they beheld all things in order,
and observed a profound silence everywhere (as they
afterwards declared to others), they thought no such
calamity had happened, but that the report was false.
So discreetly had you settled the affairs of the house at
that time, when no small confusion and disorder might
have been expected. And yet you gave this son suck
yourself, and endured the lancing of your breast to
prevent the ill effects of a contusion. These are things
worthy of a generous woman, and one that loves her
children. . . .

" Moreover, I would have you endeavor to call often
to mind that time when our daughter was not as yet
born to us, then we had no cause to complain of fortune. Then, joining that time with this, argue thus
with yourself, that we are in the same condition as
then. Otherwise, dear wife, we shall seem discontented
at the birth of our little daughter if we own that our
circumstances were better before her birth. But the

two years of her life are by no means to be forgotten
by us, but to be numbered amongst our blessings, in
that they afforded us an agreeable pleasure.   Nor must
we esteem a small good for a great evil, nor ungrate-
fully complain of fortune for what she has actually
given us, because she has not added what we wished
for.   Certainly, to speak reverently of the gods, and to
bear our lot with an even mind, without accusing fortune, always brings with it a fair reward.   .   .   .

   " But if you lament the poor girl because she died
unmarried and without offspring, you have wherewithal
to comfort yourself, in that you are defective in none
of these things, having had your share.   And those are
not small benefits where they are enjoyed.   But so long
as she is gone to a place where she feels no pain, she
has no need of our grief.   For what harm can befall us
from her when she is free from all hurt?   And surely,
the loss of great things abates its grief when it is come
to this, that there is no more ground of grief, or care
for them.   But thy Timoxena was deprived but of small
matters, for she had no knowledge but of such, neither
took she delight but in such small things.   But for that
which she never was sensible of, nor so much as once
did enter her thoughts, how can you say it is taken
from you?

   " As for what you hear others say, who persuade the
vulgar that the soul when once freed from the body,
suffers no inconvenience or evil, nor is sensible at all,
I know that you are better grounded in the doctrines

delivered down to us from our ancestors, as also in the sacred mysteries of Bacchus, than to believe such stories, for the religious symbols are well known to us who are of the fraternity. Therefore, be assured that the soul, being incapable of death, suffers in the same manner as birds that are kept in a cage. For if she has been a long time educated and cherished in the body, and by long custom has been made familiar with most things of this life, she will (though separable) return to it again, and at length enters the body; nor ceases it by new birth now and then to be entangled in the chances and events of this life. For do not think that old age is therefore evil spoken of and blamed, because it is accompanied with wrinkles, gray hairs, and weakness of body; but this is the most troublesome thing in old age, that it stains and corrupts the soul with the remembrances of things relating to the body, to which she was too much addicted; thus it bends and loves, retaining that form which it took of the body. But that which is taken away in youth, being more soft and tractable, soon returns to its native vigor and beauty, just like fire that is quenched, which, if it be forthwith kindled again, sparkles and burns out immediately.

> As soon as e'er we take one breath
> 'T were good to pass the gates of death,

before too great love of bodily and earthly things be engendered in the soul, and it become soft and tender

by being used to the body, and, as it were, by charms
and portions incorporated with it. But the truth of
this will appear in the laws and traditions, received
from our ancestors; for when children die, no libations
nor sacrifices are made for them, nor any other of those
ceremonies which are wont to be performed for the
dead. For infants have no part of earth or earthly
affections, nor do they hover or tarry about their sepul-
chres or monuments, where their dead bodies are ex-
posed. The religion of our country teaches us otherwise,
and it is an impious thing not to believe what our laws
and traditions assert, that the souls of infants pass
immediately into a better and more divine state; therefore, since it is safer to give credit to our traditions
than to call them in question, let us comply with the
custom in outward and public behavior, and let our
interior be more unpolluted, pure and holy."

JUNE.

Rose leaves and buds, the season's flowers,
Scenting afresh the summer hours,
The ruddy morn, the evening's close,
Day's labors long and night's repose.

BERRIES.

RISE with the sun, if you would keep the commandments. The sleep you get before midnight goes to virtue; after sunrise, to vice. "It is wise," says Aristotle, "to be up before daybreak, for such habit contributes to health, wealth, and wisdom." If this virtue, commended alike by antiquity and by our sense of self-respect, has fallen into discredit in modern times, it was practised by our forefathers and bore its fruits. They

"With much shorter and far sweeter sleep content,
  Vigorous and fresh about their labors went."

"He that in the morning hath heard the voice of virtue," says Confucius, "may die at night." And it were virtuous to rise early during our June mornings to breakfast on strawberries with the robins, or what were as good, partake of Leigh Hunt's delicious Essay on these berries. One tastes them from his potted pages. And his very quotations are palatable.

"My Lord of Ely, when I was last in Holburn,
  I saw good strawberries in your garden there;
  I pray you send for some of them."

An ancient may read " Concord" instead of " my Lord of Ely's " gardens, and enjoy the sight moreover of his grandson's vermilioned fingers while picking them ; the berries in no wise inferior to his Lordship's in flavor or color, and far larger in size, — that Yankee superstition. But one tastes none like the wild ones plucked fresh from the meadows of his native place, while the dews sparkled in the grasses, and the bobolink sought to decoy him from her nest there when he approached it. The lay lingers in the ear still : —

> " A single note, so sweet and low,
>   Like a full heart's overflow,
>   Forms the prelude, — but the strain
>   Gives us no sweet tone again ;
>   For the wild and saucy song
>   Leaps and skips the notes among
>   With such quick and sportive play,
>   Ne'er was merrier, madder lay."

Herrick dished his with fresh cream from his " little buttery " : —

> " You see the cream but naked is,
>   Nor dances in the eye
>   Without a strawberry,
>   Or some fine tincture like to this
>   Which draws the sight thereto."

So Milton's Eve in Eden, —

> " From many a berry and from sweet kernels pressed,
>   She tempered dulcet creams."

And Aratus, whom St. Paul quotes concerning the gods, calls the berries in aid in describing the roseate cheek of health : —

> " Fair flesh like snow with vermilion mixed,"

a line that took Goethe's fancy when composing his Theory of Colors.

Randolph, too, Ben Jonson's young friend, rides out of London with " worthy Stafford" in quest of some, —

> " Come, spur away,
>   I have no patience for a longer stay;
>   But I must go down
>   And leave the changeable air of this great town.
>   I will the country see,
>   Where old simplicity,
>   Though hid in gray,
>   Doth look more gay
>   Than foppery in plush and scarlet clad;
>   Farewell ye city wits that are
>   Almost at city war, —
>   'T is time that I grew wise when all the world is mad.

> " Here from the tree
>   We 'll cherries pluck, and pick the strawberry;
>   And every day
>   Go see the wholesome girls make hay,
>   Whose brown hath lovelier grace
>   Than any painted face
>   That I do know
>   Hyde Park can show.

> " Then full, we 'll seek a shade,
>   And hear what music 's made;

> How Philomel
> Her tale doth tell,
> And how the other birds do fill the choir,
> The thrush and blackbird lend their throats,
> Warbling melodious notes,
> We will all sports enjoy that others do desire."

The strawberry, it appears, was not restored to gardens till within a century or two back. Evelyn mentions " planting them out of the woods." I do not find it mentioned as a cultivated plant in the Greek or Roman rural authors. Phillips, in his History of Fruits, gives this pleasant account of the origin of its name. That of " an ancient practice of children threading the wild berries upon straws of grass," somewhat as rude country boys thread birds' egg-shells like beads, as ornaments for their mirrors. He says that this is still a custom in parts of England where they abound, and that so many " straws of berries " are sold for a penny, — a more picturesque style of marketing than in pottles, or boxes. Evelyn mentions the kinds common in his time : Common Wood, English, American, or Virginia, Polona, White, Ivy Red, the Green, and Scarlet.

Culpepper, in his British Herbal, says : " This plant is so well known that it needs no description. It grows in woods and is planted in gardens. It flowers in May ; the fruit ripens soon after. Venus owns the herb. The fruit, when green, is cool and dry ; but when ripe, cool and moist." He gives a list of its medical virtues, among which, he says, " the water of the berries, carefully distilled, is a remedy and cordial in the panting and beating of the heart." It were almost worth having this trouble to be cured by his strawberry cordials.

He describes the raspberry, also called thimbleberry, and ascribes to it similar medical virtues.

Of bilberries, he says there are two sorts common in England, — the black and red. The red bilberry he calls "whortleberry," and says: "The black groweth in forests, on the heath, and such like barren places. The red grows in the north parts of this land, as Lancashire, Yorkshire, etc., flowers in March and April, the fruit ripening in July and August." "Both are under the dominion of Jupiter," and, if we may believe him, are very virtuous, it being "a pity they are used no more in physic than they are." In August we gather as good in

OUR BLUEBERRY SWAMP.

" Orange groves mid-tropic lie,
   Festal for the Spaniard's eye,
   And the red pomegranate grows
   Where the luscious southwest blows;
   Myrrh and spikenard in the East
   Multiply the Persian's feast,
   And our northern wilderness
   Boasts its fruits our lips to bless.
   Wouldst enjoy a magic sight,
   And so heal vexation's spite?
   Hasten to my blueberry swamp, —
   Green o'erhead the wild bird's camp;

" Here in thickets bending low,
    Thickly piled the blueberries grow,
    Freely spent on youth and maid,
    In the deep swamp's cooling shade,
    Pluck the clusters plump and full,
    Handful after handful pull!
    Choose which path, the fruitage hangs, —
    Fear no more the griping fangs
    Of the garden's spaded stuff, —
    This is healthy, done enough.
    Pull away! the afternoon
    Dies beyond the meadow soon.
    Art thou a good citizen?
    Move into a blueberry fen;
    Here are leisure, wealth, and ease,
    Sure thy taste and thought to please,
    Drugged with nature's spicy tunes,
    Hummed upon the summer noons.

" Rich is he that asks no more
    Than of blueberries a store,
    Who can snatch the clusters off,
    Pleased with himself and them enough.
    Fame? — the chickadee is calling; —
    Love? — the fat pine cones are falling;
    Heaven? — the berries in the air, —
    Eternity — their juice so rare.
    And if thy sorrows will not fly,
    Then get thee down and softly die.
    In the eddy of the breeze,
    Leave the world beneath those trees,
    And the purple runnel's tune
    Melodize thy mossy swoon."

W. E. CHANNING.

LETTERS.

THURSDAY, 3.

"Love is the life of friendship; letters are
The life of love, the loadstones that by rare
Attractions make souls meet and melt, and mix,
As when by fire exalted gold we fix."

BUT for letters the best of our life would hardly
survive the mood and the moment Prompted by
so lively a sentiment as friendship, we commit to our
leaves what we should not have spoken. To begin
with " Dear Friend " is in itself an address which
clothes our epistle in a rhetoric the most select and
choice. We cannot write it without considering its
fitness and taxing our conscience in the matter. 'T is
coming to the confessional, leaving nothing in reserve
that falls gracefully into words. A life-long correspondence were a biography of the correspondents.
Preserve your letters till time define their value. Some
secret charm forbids committing them to the flames;
the dews of the morning may sparkle there still, and
remind one of his earlier Eden.

" Deeds are masculine, words feminine; letters are
neither," wrote Howel. Rather say, letters are both,
and better represent life than any form in literature.
Women have added the better part, the most celebrated letters having been written by women. If
your morning's letter is not answered and dispatched

forthwith, 't is doubtful if it will ever be written.   Then
there are those to whom one never writes, much as he
may wish to cultivate correspondence.   He reserves
them for personal intercourse.

I hardly know which I most enjoy, the letter I send
after my visitor, or the visit itself: the presence, the
conversation, the recollection.   Memory idealizes anticipation; our visit is made before we make it, made
afterwards, as if love were a reminiscence of pleasures
once partaken in overflowing fulness.   The visit that is
not all we anticipated is not made; we meet as idealists, if we meet at all.

> My moments are not mine, thou art in sight
> By days' engagements and the dreams of night,
> Nor dost one instant leave me free
> Forgetful of thy world and thee.

The popular superstition favors long visits.   I confess my experience has not borne out the current creed.
Compliment, of course, is of the other opinion, if we
must take her fine accents of " stay, stay longer."   But
a week's stay with an angel would hardly bear the
epithet angelic after it was over.   Fewer and farther
between.   Good things are good to keep long by temperate use.   'T is true a visitor who comes seldom should
not fly away forthwith.   And 't is a comfort in these
fast times to catch one who has a little leisure on hand,
deaf the while to the engine's whistle.   *Stay* is a charming word in a friend's vocabulary.   But if one does
not stay while staying, better let him go where he is

gone the while. One enjoys a visitor who has much leisure in him, in her especially, — likes to take his friends by sips sweetly, not at hasty draughts, as they were froth and would effervesce forthwith and subside. Who has not come from an interview as from a marriage feast, feeling " the good wine had been kept for him till *now* "?

Does it imply a refinement in delicacy that nuptial verses have no place with us in marriage ceremonies; that the service has lost the mystic associations wont to be thrown around it by our ancestors down almost to our time? Once epithalamium verses were esteemed the fairest flowers, the ornament of the occasion. If the poet sometimes overstepped modern notions of reserve, the sentiments expressed were not the less natural if more freely dealt with. Spenser, for instance, suggests the loveliest images, and with all his wealth of fancy ventures never a glimpse that a bride can blame; while Donne delights in every posture of fancy, as if he were love's attorney putting in his plea for all delights, — yet delicately, oftentimes, and on other occasions, as in these lines entitled " Love Tokens " : —

" Send me some token that my hope may live,
    Or that my ceaseless thoughts may sleep and rest;
Send me some honey to make sweet my hive,
    That in my passions I may hope the best.

I beg no ribbon wrought with thine own hands
  To knit our loves in the fantastic strain
Of new-touched youth; nor ring to show the stands
  Of our affection : — that as that's round and plain,
So should our loves meet in simplicity, —
  No, nor the corals which thy wrist infold
Laced up together in congruity
  To show our thoughts should rest in the same hold :
No, nor thy picture, though most gracious,
  And most desired since 't is like the best,
Nor witty lines which are most copious
  Within the writings which thou hast addressed :
Send me not this, nor that, to increase my store,
But swear thou think'st I love thee, and no more."

To the Lady Goodyeare he writes : —

"MADAM : — I am not come out of England if I remain in the noblest part of it, your mind. Yet I confess it is too much diminution to call your mind any part of England, or this world, since every part of even your body deserves titles to a higher dignity. No Prince would be loath to die that were assured of so fair a tomb to preserve his memory. But I have a greater advantage than this, for since there is a religion in friendship, and death in absence, to make up an entire friend there must needs be a heaven too; and there can be no heaven so proportional to that religion and that death, as your favor. And I am the gladder that it is a heaven, than it were a court, or any other high place of this world, because I am likelier to have a room there, and better, cheap. Madam, my best treasure is time, and my best employment of that (next my thoughts of thankfulness to my Redeemer) is to study good wishes for you, in which I am, by continual meditation, so learned that any creature except your own good angel, when it does you most good, might be content to come and take instruction from

> Your humble and affectionate servant,
>
> J. D.
>
> Amyens, the 7th of February, year 1611."

What delicacy of compliment, coupled with nobility of sentiment, the fresh color of flattery not less, the rhetoric so graceful. One asks if our New-England reserve has added any graces to the Elizabethan courtliness, and if any feel quite at home in its tight costumes. Is it a want of taste if one is taken with such courtly compliments, lofty appreciation of character, such stately idealism, extravagant as it may appear, and bordering on insincerity? I wish my behavior, my letters, my address, may blush becomingly, court my friends' eyes as well as affections, by coy diffidences, win by lively phrase, telling how lovely presence is. Friendship is a plant that loves the sun, — thrives ill under clouds. I know temperaments have their zones, and can excuse the frigid manner of some in whose breasts there burns a hidden flame. There is a reserve that seems to fear the affections will be frosted by exposure, if not protected from any wind of acknowledgment. If "your humble servant" is written seldomer at the end of the letter, and "Sir" and "Madam" have dropped the once "Dear" and "My Dear" — used these adjectively for ceremony's sake, — the address has lost so much warmth and all the *abandon* the words once implied. Must I withhold expressing all I would, lest

I should seem to imply more than I meant? And has one nothing personal and private to communicate? It were not unbecoming to inquire if our Puritan culture still held us in check, life and literature were under eclipse, and the shadow threatening to become central and total.

Of celebrated letters, Pliny's are among the most delightful. A perusal of them refreshes and restores the old faith in persons and the possibilities of friendship. Alas for an age, if indifferent to this antique of virtue, the fair fellowships it celebrates, in the noble names of which he gives so many illustrious examples in his charming pages. Virtue seems something to be sought, to live and die for, every accomplishment a part of it, and a possession. I confess to a feeling, as I read, so modern and consonant to ideas and designs dear to me, that for the time I seem to recover brothers and friends — if it were not egotism to say it — in the aims and ends which I have so long loved and still cherish as life's pursuit and problem. A vein of noble morality pervades these letters which renders them admirable reading for all times and ages. And his allusions to his own life and pursuits, the glimpses he gives of his friends, commend his pages to all who seek virtue and wisdom at their sources. To his friend Paternus he writes with a tenderness and humanity to which the epithet Christian would add little.

" The sickness which has lately run through my

family, and carried off several of my domestics, some
of them, too, in the prime of their years, has deeply
afflicted me.   I have two consolations, however; while
though they are not adequate to so considerable a loss,
still they are consolations.   One is, that as I have always
very readily manumized my slaves, their death does not
seem altogether immature, if they lived long enough
to receive their freedom; the other, that I have allowed
them to make a kind of will, which I observe as religiously as if they were legally entitled to that privilege.   I receive and obey their last requests as so
many absolute commands, suffering them to dispose of
their effects to whom they please; with this single re-
striction, that they leave them to some of the family,
which to persons in their station is to be considered as
a sort of commonwealth.   But though I endeavor to
acquiesce under these reflections, yet the same tenderness which led me to show them these indulgences, still
breaks out and renders me too sensitively affected by
their deaths.   However, I would not wish to be incapable of these tender impressions of humanity, though the
generality of the world, I know, look upon losses of
this kind in no other view than as a diminution of their
property, and fancy, by cherishing such an unfeeling
temper, they discover superior fortitude and philosophy.
Their fortitude and philosophy I will not dispute; but
humane, I am sure they are not; for it is the very
criterion of true manhood to feel those impressions of
sorrow which it endeavors to resist, and to admit not

9

to be above the want of consolation. But perhaps I have detained you too long upon this subject, though not so long as I would. There is a certain pleasure in giving vent to one's grief, especially when we pour out our sorrow in the bosom of a friend, who will approve, or, at least, pardon our tears. Farewell."

Again to Geminitus : —

" Have you never observed a sort of people who, though they are themselves the abject slaves of every vice, show a kind of malicious indignation against the immoral conduct of others, and are the most severe to those whom they most resemble? Yet surely a beauty of disposition, even in persons who have least occasion for clemency themselves, is of all virtues the most becoming. The highest of character in my estimation, is His, who is as ready to pardon the moral errors of mankind as if he were every day guilty of some himself, and at the same time as cautious of committing a fault as if he never forgave one. It is a rule, then, which we should upon all occasions, both private and public, most religiously observe, *to be inexorable to our own failings, while we treat those of the rest of the world with tenderness, not excepting even those who forgive none but themselves,* remembering always that the humane, and, therefore, as well as upon other accounts, the great Thrasea, used frequently to say, ' *He who hates vice hates mankind.*' You will ask me, perhaps, who it is that has given occasion to these reflections. You must know a certain person lately, — but of that when we meet, — though, upon second thoughts, not even then, lest while I condemn and expose his conduct, I should act counter to that maxim I particularly recommend· Whoever, therefore, and whatever he is, shall remain in silence ; for though there may be some use, perhaps, in setting a mark upon the man, for the sake of example, there will be more, however, in sparing him, for the sake of humanity."

Again : —

" There are, it seems," he writes to his friend Septitius, " certain persons who in your company have blamed me, as being upon all occasions too lavish in commendation of my friends. I not only acknowledge the charge, but glory in it ; for, can there be a nobler error than an overflowing benevolence? But still, who are these, let me ask, that are better acquainted with my friends than I am myself? Yet, grant there are such, why will they deny me the satisfaction of so pleasing an error? For, supposing my friends deserve not the high encomiums I give them, certainly I am happy in believing they do. Let them recommend, then, this ungenerous discernment to those who imagine (and their number is not inconsiderable) that they show their judgment when they indulge their censure. As for myself, they will never persuade me that I can love my friends too well."

How amiable and just are sentiments like these rendering odious the carping censure and ill-natured criticism which finds free currency between those who, while meeting as acquaintances, perhaps affecting friendship for each other, yet speak disparagingly, and are loath to acknowledge the merit which they see in each other's character and acquirements. It is safer, and certainly more becoming, to overpraise than to undervalue and dispraise another. Faults are apparent enough, and, for the most part, superficial; in the atmosphere of affection and respect they fall away presently and disappear altogether, while virtues may be too deep sometimes and delicate in expression to be recognized readily by those who seek for blemishes rather. Modest praise is the freshest and purest atmosphere for modest virtue to thrive in and come to maturity. And the most exalted qualities of character admiration alone brings into the relief that discloses their proportions and reveals their lustre. A certain sentiment of worship insinuates itself into our affections for a near and dear friend; and while endearing us the more, yet holds us at the distance of reverence and of self-respect that belongs to the noblest friendships. 'T is the poverty of life that renders friendship poor and cold. I am drawn to one who, while I approach yet seems distant still; whose personality has a quality so commanding as to forbid a familiarity not justified by affection and reason alike, and whom I never quite come up to, but yet is akin to me in the attributes that win my regard and insure my affection. A good man is a bashful man; he affects all who come within his influence with that grace.

Do not the gods blush in descending to meet alike our
affections and our eyes?

"The eldest god is still a child."

BOOKS.

TUESDAY, 8.

NEXT to a friend's discourse, no morsel is more
delicious than a ripe book, a book whose flavor is
as refreshing at the thousandth tasting as at the first.
Books when friends weary, conversation flags, or nature
fails to inspire. The best books appeal to the deepest
in us and answer the demand. A book loses if wanting
the personal element, gains when this is insinuated, or
comes to the front occasionally, blending history with
mythology.

My favorite books have a personality and complexion
as distinctly drawn as if the author's portrait were
framed into the paragraphs and smiled upon me as I
read his illustrated pages. Nor could I spare them
from my table or shelves, though I should not open the
leaves for a twelvemonth; — the sight of them, the
knowledge that they are within reach, accessible at
any moment, rewards me when I invite their company.
Borrowed books are not mine while in hand. I
covet ownership in the contents, and fancy that he who
is conversant with these is the rightful owner, and
moreover, that the true scholar owes to scholars a

catalogue of his chosen volumes, that they may learn
from whence his entertainment during leisure moments.
Next to a personal introduction, a list of one's favorite
authors were the best admittance to his character and
manners. His library were not voluminous. He might
specify his favorites on his fingers, and spare the
printer's type.

" Books have many charming qualities to such as
know how to choose them." And without Plutarch,
no library were complete.

Can we marvel at his fame, or overestimate the surpassing merits of his writings? It seems as I read as
if none before, none since, had written lives, as if he
alone were entitled to the name of biographer, — such
intimacy of insight is his, laying open the springs of
character, and through his parallels portraying his times
as no historian had done before : not Plato, even, in the
livelier way of dialogue with his friends. Then his
morals are a statement of the virtues for all times. And
I read the list of his lost writings, not without a sense
of personal wrong done to me, with emotions akin to
what the merchant might feel in perusing the bill of
freight after the loss of his vessel. Hercules, Hesiod,
Pindar, Leonidas, Scipio, Augustus, Claudius, Epami-
nondas, minds of mark, all these and other precious
pieces gone to the bottom : his books on the Academy
of Plato, The Philosophers, and many more of this
imperial freight, to be read by none now. Still, there
remains so much to be grateful for ; so many names

surviving to perpetuate virtue and all that is splend.
in fame, with his own. I for one am his debtor, not for
noble examples alone, but for portraits of the possibilities of virtue, and all that is dearest in friendship,
in his attractive pages. It is good exercise, good medicine, the reading of his books, — good for to-day, as in
times it was preceding ours, salutary reading for all
times.

Montaigne also comes in for a large share of the
scholar's regard. Opened anywhere, his page is sensible, marrowy, quotable. He may be taken up, too, and
laid aside carelessly without loss, so inconsequent is his
method, and he so careless of his wealth. Professing
nature and honesty of speech, his page has the suggestions of the landscape, is good for striking out in any
direction, suited to any mood, sure of yielding variety
of information, wit, entertainment, — not to be commanded, to be sure, without grave abatements, to be
read with good things growing side by side with things
not such and tasting of the apple. Still, with every
abatement, his book is one of the ripest and mellowest,
and, bulky as it is, we wish there were more of it. He
seems almost the only author whose success warrants in
every stroke of his pen his right to guide it: he of the
men of letters, the prince of letters; since writing of
life, he omits nothing of its substance, but tells all with
a courage unprecedented. His frankness is charming.
So his book has indescribable attractions, being as
it were a Private Book, — his diary self-edited, and

offered with an honesty that wins his readers, he never having done bestowing his opulent hospitalities on him, gossiping sagely, and casting his wisdom in sport to any who care for it. Everywhere his page is alive and rewarding, and we are disappointed at finding his book comes to an end like other books.

Lord Herbert's Autobiography is a like example of sincerity and naturalness. If he too often play the cavalier, and is of a temper that brooks not the suspicion of insult, he is equally eager to defend when friendship or humanity render it a duty. The brothers, Edward and George, were most estimable characters. To George how largely are we in debt for his sacred verses, the delight and edification of the saints wherever they are known. Add Vaughan and Crashaw. And making due allowance for the time when Herrick's verses were written, his temptation to suit the tastes of courtiers and kings, his volumes contain much admirable poetry, tempered with religious devotion. He wrote sweet and virtuous verse, with lines here and there that should not have been written. But he is an antedote to the vice in his lines, and may well have place in the scholar's library with Donne, Daniel, Cowley, Shakespeare, and contemporaries.

If one would learn the titles and gain insight into the contents of the best books in our literature, let him track Coleridge in his readings and notes as these have been collected and published in his Literary Remains and Table Talk. He explored the wide field of litera-

ture and philosophy, and brought to light richer spoils
than any scholar of his time, or since. His reading
was not only choice, but miscellaneous. Nothing of
permanent value appears to have escaped his searching
glance, and his criticisms on books are among the most
valuable contributions to British letters. He knew how
to read to get and give the substance of the book in
sprightly comment and annotation on the text. His
judgments are final and exhaustive. To follow him
were an education in itself.

One's diary is attractive reading, and productive, if
he have the art of keeping one.

Thoreau wrote in his : —

" I set down such choice experiences that my own
writings may inspire me, and at last I may make
wholes of parts. Certainly it is a distinct profession
to rescue from oblivion and to fix the sentiments and
thoughts which visit all men, more or less, generally,
and that the contemplation of the unfinished picture
may suggest its harmonious completion. Associate
reverently and as much as you can with your loftiest
thoughts. Each thought that is welcomed and recorded
is a nest-egg by the side of which another will be laid.
Thoughts accidentally thrown together become a frame
in which more may be developed and exhibited. Perhaps this is the main value of a habit of writing or
keeping a journal, — that is, we remember our best
draught, and stimulate ourselves. My thoughts are
my company. They have a certain individuality and

separate existence, large personality. Having by chance recorded a few disconnected thoughts and then brought them into juxtaposition, they suggest a whole new field in which it is possible to labor and think. Thought begets thought. I have a commonplace-book for facts, and another for poetry. But I find it difficult always to preserve the vague distinctions which I had in my mind, for the most interesting and beautiful facts are so much the more poetry, — and that is their success. They are translated from earth to heaven. I see that if my facts were sufficiently vital and significant, perhaps transmuted more into the substance of the human mind, I should need but one book of poetry to contain them all.

"I do not know but thoughts written down thus in a journal might be printed in the same form with greater advantage than if the related ones were brought together into separate essays. They are allied to life, and can be seen by the reader not to be far-fetched; thus, more simple, less artful. I feel that in the other case, I should have a proper form for my sketches. Here facts and names and dates communicate more than we suspect. Whether the flower looks better in the nosegay than in the meadow where it grew, and we had to wet our feet to get it? Is the scholastic air any advantage? Perhaps I can never find so good a setting for thoughts as I shall thus have taken them out of. The crystal never sparkles more brightly than in the cavern. The world have always liked best the fable with the moral. The children could read the fable alone. The grown-up read both. The truth so told has the best advantages of the most abstract statement, for it is not the less universally applicable. Where else will you ever find the true cement for your thoughts? How will you ever rivet them together without leaving the marks of your file?

"Yet Plutarch did not so. Montaigne did not so. Men have written travels in this form; but perhaps no man's daily life has been rich enough to be journalized. Yet one's life should be so active and progressive as to be a journey. But I am afraid to travel much, or to famous places, lest it might completely dissipate the mind. Then I am sure that what we observe at home, if we observe anything, is of more importance than what we observe abroad. The far-fetched is of least value. What we observe in travelling are to some extent the accidents of the body; but what we observe when sitting at home are in the same proportion phenomena of the mind itself. A wakeful night will yield as much thought as a long journey. If I try thoughts by their quality, not their quantity, I may find that a restless night will yield more than the longest journey."

These masterpieces, Thoreau's Diaries, are a choice mingling of physical and metaphysical elements. They show the art above art which was busied about their composition. They come near fulfilling the highest ends of expression; the things seen become parts of the describer's mind, and speak through his Person. Quick with thought, his sentences are colored and con- solidated therein by his plastic genius.

Of gifts, there seems none more becoming to offer a friend than a beautiful book, books of verse especially. How exquisite these verses of Crashaw's, " Addressed to a Lady with a Prayer Book."

" Lo, here a little volume, but great book,
        Fear it not, sweet,
        It is no hypocrite,
    Much larger in itself, than in its look.

" It is, in one rich handful, heaven and all
    Heaven's royal hosts encamp'd, thus small,
    To prove that true schools used to tell
    A thousand angels in one point can dwell.

" 'T is Love's great artillery
    Which here contracts itself and comes to lie
    Close couched in your white bosom, and from thence
    As from a snowy fortress of defence
    Against the ghostly foe to take your part,
    And fortify the hold of your chaste heart.

" It is the armory of light,
    Let constant use but keep it bright,
        You 'll find it yields
    To holy hands and humble hearts,
        More swords and shields
    Than sin hath snares, or hell hath darts.

Only be sure
The hands be pure
That hold these weapons, and the eyes
Those of turtles, chaste and true,
 Wakeful and wise.

" Here is a friend shall fight for you;
Hold this book before your heart,
 Let prayer alone to play his part.

 " But O! the heart
 That studies this high art,
 Must be a sure housekeeper,
 And yet no sleeper.

" Dear soul. be strong,
Mercy will come ere long,
And bring her bosom full of blessings;
 Flowers of never-fading graces
To make immortal dressings
 For worthy souls, whose wise embraces
Store up themselves for him, who is alone
The spouse of virgins, and the Virgin's Son.

" But if the noble bridegroom when he come
Shall find the wandering heart from home,
 Leaving her chaste abode
 To gad abroad
Amongst the gay mates of the god of flies,
To take her pleasures, and to play
 And keep the devil's holiday;
To dance in the sunshine of some smiling
 But beguiling
Spear of sweet and sugared lies;

Some slippery pair
Of false, perhaps as fair,
Flattering, but forswearing eyes,
Doubtless some other heart
 Will get the start,
 And stepping in before,
Will take possession of the sacred store
 Of hidden sweets and holy joys,
 Words which are not heard with ears
 (Those tumultuous shops of noise),
 Effectual whispers, whose still voice
The soul itself more feels than hears;
Amorous languishments, luminous trances,
 Sights which are not seen with eyes;
Spiritual and soul-piercing glances,
Whose pure and subtle lightning flies
Home to the heart and sets the house on fire,
And melts it down in sweet desire,
 Yet doth not stay
To ask the window's leave to pass that way.
An hundred thousand loves and graces,
 And many a mystic thing
 Which the divine embraces,
Of the dear spouse of spirits with them will bring,
 For which it is no shame
That dull mortality must not know a name.

Of all this hidden store
Of blessings, and ten thousand more,
 If when he come
He find the heart from home,
Doubtless he will unload
Himself some otherwhere,
 And pour abroad
 His precious sweets
On the fair soul whom first he meets."

SPECULATIVE PHILOSOPHY.

Thursday, 10.

THE first number of Volume III. of the "Journal of Speculative Philosophy" comes to hand, printed in fair type, with promise of attracting attention from thinkers at home and abroad. And it is a significant fact that the most appreciative notice yet taken of this Journal comes from Germany, and is written by the President of the Berlin Philosophical Society. Nor less remarkable that this first attempt to popularize Philosophy, so far as practicable, should date from the West, and show an ability in dealing with speculative questions that may well challenge the attainments of thinkers everywhere, — the translations showing a ripe scholarship, and covering almost the whole range of historic thinking.*

---

* "Nothing is more interesting in the history of the human mind than the tendency of enlightened souls in all ages to gather in clusters, as in the material world crystallization goes on by the gathering of individual atoms about one axis of formation. Thus the schools of Greek Philosophy, the Pythagorean, the Eleatic, the Peripatetic, the Alexandrian, were human crystallizations about a central idea, and generally in a given locality, — as Samos, Athens, or the Lucanian city of Elea, where Zeno learned lessons of Parmenides, and whence they both journeyed to Athens in the youth of Socrates, and held their "Radical Club" at the house of Pythodorus in the Ceramicus. The Schoolmen and the Mystics of the middle ages clustered together in the same way about Abelard. Thomas Aquinas, Occam, Gerson, Giardano Bruno, the early Italian poets, rally in groups in the same way; so do the Elizabethan Dramatists, the Puritan Politicians, the English Platonists. Coming nearer our own time, there are the Lake Poets of England, the Weimar circle of genius, in Germany, the Transcendental Idealists in

England, too, has at last found a metaphysician that Coleridge would have accepted and prized. And the more that he follows himself in introducing philosophy from Germany into Britain. James Hutchison Stirling's fervor and strength in advocating Hegel's ideas command the highest respect. Having had Schelling's expositor in Coleridge, we now have Hegel's in Stirling ; and, in a spirit of catholicity shown to foreign thought unexpected in an Englishman, promising not a little in the way of qualifying favorably the metaphysics of Britain. Nothing profound nor absolute can be expected from minds of the type of Mill, Herbert Spencer, and the rest, — if not hostile, at least

---

Concord and Boston, and finally, the German American Philosophers of St. Louis, concerning whom we now speak. In all these Schools and Fellowships of the human soul, a common impulse, aided by accident of locality and other circumstances, trivial only in appearance, has led to the formation of that strictest bond, the friendship of united aspirations. New England has so long been considered the special home of ideas, that it may surprise one to learn that St. Louis, on the Mississippi, has become the focus of a metaphysical *renasissance;* yet such it has become. A few Germans, New Englanders, and Western men gathered there, having found each other out, began to meet, expatiate, and confer about Kant and Hegel, Fichte, and Sir William Hamilton. Soon they formed a Philosophical Society, and by and by, having accumulated many manuscripts, they began to publish a Magazine of "Speculative Philosophy." At first, this publication came out semi-occasionally, but finally settled down into a regular Quarterly, with contributors on both sides of the Atlantic, and from various schools of metaphysical thought. The January number is, indeed, a remarkable production. Every article is good, and most of them profound ; no such collection of striking varieties of philosophic thought has been made public for a long time as this. The Journal is edited by William T. Harris, LL.D., Superintendent of the Public Schools of St. Louis."

F. B. SANBORN,
in " Springfield Republican," March, 1869.

indifferent to and incapable of idealism; naturalists rather than metaphysicians. It will be a most hopeful indication if Stirling's book, the "Secret of Hegel," find students among his countrymen. Cavilling there will be, of course, misapprehension, much nonsense uttered concerning Hegel's Prime Postulates. But what was thought out fairly in Germany, must find its way and prompt comprehension in England; if not there, then here in New England, out of whose heart a fresh philosophy should spring forth, to which the German Hegel shall give impulse and furtherance. The work has already begun, with Harris's publishing the thoughts of the world's thinkers, himself familiar with the best of all thinking. I look for a more flowing, inspiring type of thought, Teutonic as Greek, of a mystic coloring transcending Boehme, Swedenborg, and freed from the biblicisms of the schools of our time. Hegel's secret is that of pure thought akin with that of Parmenides, Plato, Aristotle, the ancient masters in philosophy. The One is One out of whose womb the Not One is born to perish perpetually at its birth. Whoso pronounces PERSON apprehensively, speaks the secret of all things, and holds the key to all mysteries in nature and spirit.

For further encouragement, moreover, we are promised a translation of the complete works of Plotinus, by a learned contributor to the "Journal," who has qualifications for that service unsurpassed, perhaps, by any on this side of the Atlantic.

He writes from St. Louis : —

" I have tried my hand on Plotinus, and find it easy to render the text into modern philosophical phraseology. Until lately I have been unable to procure a good critical edition of the Greek philosopher. And now, if my energies are spared, a translation of his entire works is not very far in the future." *

It were a good test of one's aptitude for metaphysical studies, his appreciation of Plotinus. Profound as any predecessor of the Platonic school of idealism, he had the remarkable merit of treating ideas in a style at once transparent and subtle, dealing with these as if they were palpable things, such was his grasp of thought and felicity in handling. His themes are of universal concernment at all times. Promoting a catholic and manly method, his books were good correctives of any exclusiveness still adhering in our schools of science and divinity, while the tendencies of his time, as in ours, were towards comparative studies.

A like tendency appeared, also, in England in the studies of the British Platonists, or Latitudinarians, — Dr. Henry More, Dr. Cudworth, Dr. Rust, Norris, Glanvil, John Smith, whose writings deserve a place in theological libraries, and the study of divines especially.

Norris thus praises his friend Dr. More, whose works had high repute and were much studied in his day : —

---

* His works are comprised in fifty-four books, which his disciple Porphyry divided into six Enneads, assigning, agreeably to the meaning of the word, nine books to every Ennead. Thomas Taylor translated parts of these only.

" Others in learning's chorus bear their part,
  And the great work distinctly share ;
  Thou, our great catholic professor art,
  All science is annexed to thy unerring chair ;
  Some lesser synods of the wise
  The Muses kept in universities ;
  But never yet till in thy soul
  Had they a council œcumenical :
  An abstract they'd a mind to see
  Of all their scattered gifts, and summed them up in thee.
  Thou hast the arts whole Zodiac run,
  And fathom'st all that here is known ;
  Strange restless curiosity,
  Adam himself came short of thee, —
  He tasted of the fruit, thou bearest away the tree."

And More writes of Plotinus : —

> " Who such things did see,
> Even in the tumult that few can arrive
> Of all are named from philosophy,
> To that high pitch or to such secrets dive." *

---

* "It would make a most delightful and instructive essay," says Coleridge, "to draw up a critical, and, where possible, biographical account of the Latitudinarian party at Cambridge, from the reign of James I to the latter half of Charles II. The greater number were Platonists, so called, at least, and such they believed themselves to be, but more truly Plotinists. Thus Cudworth, Dr. Jackson (chaplain of Charles I and Vicar of Newcastle upon Tyne), Henry More, John Smith, and some others (Norris, Glanvil). Jeremy Taylor was a Gassendist, and, as far as I know, he is the only exception. They were alike admirers of Grotius, which, in Taylor, was consistent with the tone of all his philosophy. The whole party, however, and a more amiable never existed, were scared and disgusted into this by the catachrestic language and the skeleton half truths of the systematic divines of the synod of Dort on the one hand, and by the sickly broodings of the Pietists and Solo-

PLOTINUS.

Plotinus was by birth an Egyptian, a native of Sycopolis. He died at the conclusion of the second year of the reign of M. Aurelius Flavius Claudius, at the age of sixty-six. On his friend Eustochius coming from a distance and approaching him when dying, he said : " As yet I have expected you, and now I endeavor that my divine part may return to that divine nature which flourishes throughout the universe."

Taylor says of him, " He was a philosopher preeminently distinguished for the strength and profundity of his intellect, and the purity and elevation of his life. He was wise without the usual mixture of human darkness, and great without the general combination of human weakness and imperfection. He seems to have left the orb of light solely for the benefit of mankind, that he might teach them how to repair the ruin contracted by their exile from good, and how to return to their true country and legitimate kindred allies. I do not mean that he descended into mortality for unfolding the sublimest truths to the multitude, for this would

mon's Song preachers on the other. What they all wanted was a pre-inquisition into the mind, as part organ, part constituent, of all knowledge, — an examination of the scales and weights and measures themselves abstracted from the objects to be weighed or measured by them; in short, a transcendental æsthetic, logic, and noetic. Lord Herbert was at the entrance of, nay, already some paces within, the shaft and adit of the mine; but he turned abruptly back, and the honor of establishing a complete προπαιδεία (Organon) of philosophy was reserved for Immanuel Kant, a century or more afterwards."— *Lit. Remains,* iii. 416.

have been a vain and ridiculous attempt, since their eyes, as Plato justly observes, are not strong enough to look at truth. But he came as a guide to the few who are born with a divine destiny, and are struggling to gain the lost region of light, but know not how to break the fetters by which they are detained; who are impatient to leave the obscure cavern of sense, where all is delusion and shadow, and to ascend to the realms of intellect, where all is substance and reality."

His biographers speak of him with the truest admiration. He was foreign from all sophistical ostentation and pride, and conducted himself in the company of disputants with the same freedom and ease as in his familiar discourses; for true wisdom, when it is deeply possessed, gives affability and modesty to the manners, illumines the countenance with a divine serenity, and diffuses over the whole external form an air of dignity and ease. Nor did he hastily disclose to every one the logical necessities latent in his conversation. He was strenuous in discourse, and powerful in discovering what was appropriate. While he was speaking, there was every indication of the predominance of intellect in his conceptions. The light of it diffused itself over his countenance, which was indeed, at all times, lovely, but was then particularly beautiful; a certain attenuated and dewy moisture appeared on his face, and a pleasing mildness shone forth. Then, also, he exhibited a gentleness in receiving questions, and demonstrated a vigor uncommonly robust in their solution.

He was rapidly filled with what he read, and having in a few words given the meaning of a profound theory, he arose. He borrowed nothing from others, his conceptions being entirely his own, and his theories original. He could by no means endure to read twice what he had written. Such, indeed, was the power of his intellect, that when he had once conceived the whole disposition of his thoughts from the beginning to the end, and had afterwards committed them to writing, his composition was so connected, that he appeared to be merely transcribing a book. Hence he would discuss his domestic affairs without departing from the actual intention of his mind, and at one and the same time transact the necessary negotiations of friendship, and preserve an uninterrupted survey of the things he had proposed to consider. In consequence of this uncommon power of intellection, when he returned to writing, after the departure of the person with whom he had been conversing, he did not review what he had written; and yet he so connected the preceding with the subsequent conceptions, as if his composition had not been interrupted. Hence, he was at the same time present with others and with himself; so that the self-converted energy of his intellect was never remitted, except in sleep, which his admirable temperance in meats and drinks, and his constant conversion to intellect, contributed in no small measure to expel. Though he was attentive to his pupils and the necessary concerns of life, the intellectual energy of his soul while he was awake never suffered any interruption from externals, nor any remission of vigor. He was likewise extremely mild in his manners, and easy of access to all his friends and adherents. Hence, so great was his philosophic urbanity, that though he resided at Rome six and twenty years, and had been the arbitrator in many litigious causes which he amicably dissolved, yet he had scarcely an enemy throughout that vast and illustrious city. Indeed, he was so highly esteemed, not only by the senate and people of Rome, that the Emperor Galienus and his wife Salonica honored his person and reverenced his doctrine; and relying on his benevolence, requested that a city in Campania, which had been formerly destroyed, might be restored, and rendered a fit habitation for philosophers, and besides this, that it might be governed by the laws of Plato, and called Platonopolis.

IDEAL CULTURE.

THURSDAY, 17.

THE new courses of lectures at Harvard University are advertised by the new President. They are a novelty in our college culture. A marked peculiarity is the announcement of a course to be given by Emerson, on the Natural History of Intellect; by Dr. Hedge, on Theism, Atheism, and Pantheism; and by J. Eliot Cabot, on Kant. The course, or any part of it, is open " to graduates, teachers, and other competent persons, men or women."

It is hoped, also, that Hutchison Stirling may be added to the list of lecturers, — an acquisition certainly that Harvard should be proud to secure, both for its own and the credit of metaphysical studies on this side of the Atlantic.

The English mind seems to have held aloof from pure metaphysics, — from German Idealism, especially. Berkeley, its finest thinker since Bacon, was for a long time misapprehended, if, indeed, he is fairly appreciated as yet. Boehme, Kant, Schelling, were unknown till Coleridge introduced their ideas to the notice of his contemporaries — Carlyle those of Goethe, and the great scholars of Germany.

" Great, indeed," says Coleridge, " are the obstacles which an English metaphysician has to encounter. Amongst his most respectable and intelligent judges, there will be many who have devoted their attention exclusively to the concerns and interests of human life, and who bring with them to the perusal of philosophical systems, an habitual aversion to all speculations, the utility and application of which are not evident and immediate.

" There are others whose prejudices are still more formidable, inasmuch as they are grounded in their moral feelings and religious principles, which had been alarmed and shocked by the injurious and pernicious tenets defended by Hume, Priestley, and the French Fatalists, or Necessitarians, some of whom had perverted metaphysical reasonings to the denial of the mysteries, and, indeed, of all the peculiar doctrines of Christianity; and others, to the subversion of all distinctions between right and wrong.

" A third class profess themselves friendly to metaphysics, and believe that they are themselves metaphysicians. They have no objection to system and termology, provided it be the method and nomenclature to which they have been familiarized in the writings of Locke, Hume, Hartley, Condillac, or, perhaps, Dr. Reid and Professor Stewart.

" But the worst and widest impediment remains. It is the predominance of a popular philosophy, at once the counterfeit and mortal enemy of all true and manly metaphysical research. It is that corruption introduced by certain immethodical aphorising Eclectics, who, dismissing, not only all system, but all logical consequence, pick and choose whatever is most plausible and showy; who select whatever words can have semblance of sense attached to them, without the least expenditure of thought; in short, whatever may enable men to talk of what they do not understand, with a careful avoidance of everything that might awaken them to a moment's suspicion of their ignorance."

Fifty years and more have passed since this criticism was written; and, with slight change of names for similar things, it still holds for the popular estimate put upon metaphysics by too many scholars of our time. If Coleridge, Schelling, Hegel, and the rest, are still held in disregard by persons in chairs of philosophy, we may infer the kind of culture which the universities favor. What he also said of intellectual culture in his country and time, holds scarcely less true as regards ours; and this in a republic, too, which in theory educates all its citizens.

" I am greatly deceived if one preliminary to an efficient popular education be not the recurrence to a more manly discipline of the intellect on the part of the learned themselves; in short, a thorough recasting of the moulds in which the minds of our gentry, the characters of our future landowners, magistrates, and senators, are to receive their shape and fashion. What treasures of practical wisdom would be once more brought to open day by the solution of the problem. Suffice it for the present to hint the master thought.

" The first man on whom the light of an Idea dawned, did in that same moment receive the spirit and credentials of a lawgiver. And as long as man shall exist, so long will the possession of that antecedent — the maker and master of all profitable experience, which exists in the power of an idea — be the one lawful qualification for all dominion in the world of the senses. Without this, experience itself is but a Cyclops walking backwards under the fascinations of the past; and we are indebted to a lucky coincidence of outward circumstances and contingencies, least of all to be calculated on in a time like the present, if this one-eyed experience does not seduce its worshippers into practical anachronisms. But, alas! the halls of the old philosophers have been so long deserted, that we circle them at shy distance, as the haunt of phantoms and chimeras. The sacred grave of Academus is held in like regard with the unfruitful trees in the shadowy world of Maro, that had a dream attached to every leaf. The very terms of ancient wisdom are worn out; or, far worse, stamped as baser metal; and whoever should have the hardihood to re-proclaim its solemn truths, must commence with a glossary."

The Dialectic, or Method of the Mind, constitutes the basis of all culture. Without a thorough discipline in this, our schools and universities give but a showy and superficial training. The knowledge of mind is the beginning of all knowledge; without this a theology is baseless, the knowledge of God impossible. Modern education has not dealt with these deeper questions of life and being. It has the future in which to prove its power of conducting a Cultus, answering to the discipline of the Greek thinkers, Pythagoras, Plato, Aristotle.

As yet we deal with mind with far less certainty than with matter; the realm of intellect having been less explored than the world of the senses, and both are treated conjecturally rather than absolutely. When we come to perceive that Intuition is the primary postulate of all intelligence, most questions now perplexing and obscure will become transparent; the lower imperfect methods then take rank where they belong and are available. The soul leads the senses; the reason the understanding; imagination the memory; instinct and intuition include and prompt the Personality entire.

The categories of imagination are the poet's tools; those of the reason, the implements of the naturalist. The dialectic philosopher is master of both. The tools to those only who can handle them skilfully. All others but gash themselves and their subject, at best. Ask not a man of understanding to solve a problem in metaphysics. He has neither wit, weights, nor scales for the task. But a man of reason or of imagination solves readily the problems of understanding the moment these are fairly stated. Ideas are solvents of all mysteries, whether in matter or mind.

> 'T is clear
> Mind's sphere
> Is not here;
> The Ideal guest
> In ceaseless quest
> Pursues the Best:
> The very Better
> The while her fetter,
> Her desire
> Higher, still higher;
> Ever is fleeing
> Past Seeming to Being;
> Nor doth the sight content itself with seeing,
> As forms emerge they fast from sense are fleeing,
> Things but appear to vanish into Being.

So the Greeks represented thought in their winged god, Hermes, as the father of speech and messenger of intelligence; they conceiving the visible world as a globe of forms, whereby objects of thought were pictured to sense, and held forth to fancy,—a geometry of ideas, a rhetoric of images.

Sallying forth into nature, the mind clothes its ideas in fitting images, and thus reflects itself upon the understanding. Things are symbols of thoughts, and nature the mind's dictionary.

> Mind omnipresent is,
> All round about us lies,
> To fashion forth itself
> In thought and ecstacy,
> In fancy and surprise,
> Things with ideas fraught,
> And nature our dissolving thought.

GOETHE.

WEDNESDAY, 23.

"As good
Not write as not be understood."

YET the deepest truths are best read between the lines, and, for the most part, refuse to be written. Who tells all tells falsely. There are untold subtleties in things seen as unseen. Only the idealist touches the core of their secret tenderly, and extracts the mystery; Nature, like the coy Isis, disclosing these to none else. Most edifying is the author who suggests, and leaves to his reader the pleasure and profit of following his thought into its various relations with the whole of things, thus stimulating him to explore matters to their issues. The great masters have observed this fine law, and of modern scholars especially Goethe.

For whether considered as poet or naturalist, he is our finest example of the reverent faith in nature and tenderness of treatment that becomes her student and devotees. And hence the rich spoils and prime suggestions with which he charms and rewards in his books. Wooed in this spirit, nature vouchsafed him the privilege of reading her secrets. An eye-witness of the facts, he had the magic pen to portray them as they rose midway between matter and mind, there caught them lovingly and held them forth in intertwisted myths and gay marriages to the sense and sentiment of his reader. Writing faithfully to the form of things, he yet had a finer moral than these could deliver; the vein of quiet mysticism in which he delighted, giving a graceful charm to the writing. How finely his senses symbolized his thought, and his eye how Olympian! What subtle perception of the contraries in character! He has treated the strife of the Worst for the Best, the problem of evil, more cunningly than any; than Moses; than the author of Job of Uz; than Milton, the Puritan, fitted as he was alike by birth and culture to deal with this world fable, — his faith in nature being so entire, his rare gifts at instant command for rendering perfect copies of what he saw, and loved to represent in its truthfulness to sense and soul alike. A seer of Spirit, the draughtsman of guile; to him sat the demons gladly, and he sketched their likenesses, — portraits of the dualities he knew so well; the same with which most are too familiar; the drama of the temptation being coeval with man, the catastrophe thus far repeated disastrously, the striving of the Many against the One, the world-spirit bribing the will, proffering the present delights for the future pains. Ah! could he but have found himself in the One, whom, with such surpassing skill he individualized, but failed to impersonate. His aloofness from life, his residence in the Many, his inability to identify himself with the whole of things, — this duplicity of genius denied him free admittance to unity. Cunning he was, not wise in the simplicity of wisdom. As the Fates conceived, so they slew him, yet by subtleties so siren, as to persuade him of an immortality not theirs to bestow. All he was, his Faust celebrates — admitted to heaven, as Goethe to glory, without the fee that opens honestly its gates.

Oh, artist of beauty! Couldst thou but have been equal to portray the Spirit of spirits as cunningly as of Matter! But it was the temper of that age of transition, and thou wast its priest and poet.

But whatever his deficiencies, he has been one of the world's teachers, and is to be for some time to come. The spirit and movement of an age are embodied in his books, and one reads with a growing reverence at every perusal of the mind that saw and has portrayed the world-spirit so well. If not the man complete that in our admiration of his genius we could desire, he yet was faithful to the law of his pen, and therewith justifies his existence to mankind. Nor do I find any of his contemporaries who made as much of this human life during his century. " Light, more light ! " With this request he passed behind the clouds into the fullest radiance.

CARLYLE.

The ancients accepted in good faith the sway of Fate, or Temperament, in their doctrine of Destinies, hereby signifying that duplicity or polarity of forces operative in man's Will by which his personal freedom is abridged, if not overridden. Nor does it appear that they conceived deliverance possible from this dread Nemesis of existence ; it was wrought into the substance of their tragedies, binding matter and mind alike in chains. If the modern thought professes to be freed from this Old Fatalism, it practically admits it, nevertheless ; man's will being still bound in fetters by inexorable powers, which his Choice can neither propitiate nor overcome. If Goethe treats the matter more forcibly, sharply, his dealing differs but in form from the Pagan ; man is the spoil of the demons still. Satan is suppressed for the moment to be victorious in the end.

Carlyle only renders it the more inexorable and dismaying by all his wealth of thought, force of illustration, his formidable historical figures, dramatic genius. It is force pitted against force that he celebrates throughout his embattled pages; a victim himself with his heroes, yet like them never the victor; all irritants, but not quellers of the demon; fixed forces in transition times.

Only seen from this, his habitual standpoint and outlook, is he justified as the consistent realist, holding fast his faith in the actual facts of the world, their rigorous following to the remotest issues, — the most heroic of thinkers. What if, with these dread convictions and insights of his, he paint out of all keeping with the actual facts; he is following logically his persuasions of the destinies that sway human concerns, abating not an iota of the letter of the text of the dread decalogue, whether for the wicked or the weak; defending his view of the right at all costs whatsoever. Justice first, mercy afterwards. His books opened anywhere show him berating the wrong he sees, but seldom the means of removing. There is ever the same melancholy advocacy of work to be done under the dread master: force of strokes, the right to rule and be ruled, the dismal burden. He rides his Leviathan as fiercely as did his countryman, Hobbes; can be as truculent and abusive. Were he not thus fatally in earnest, we should take him for the harlequin he often seems, not seeing the sorrowing sadness thus playing off its load in this grotesque mirth, this scornful irony of his; he painting in spite of himself his portraits in the warmth of admiration, the blaze of wrath, giving us mythology for history mostly.

Yet with what breadth of perspective he paints these! strength of outline, the realism appalling, the egotism enormous, — all history showing in the background of his one figure, Carlyle, — Burns, Goethe, Richter, Mirabeau, Luther, Cromwell, Frederick, — all dashed from his flashing pen, — heads of himself alike in their unlikeness, prodigiously individual, wilful, some of them monstrous; all Englishmen, too, with their egregious prejudices, prides; no patience, no repose in any. He brandishes his truncheon through his pages with an adroitness that renders it unsafe for any, save the few wielding weapons of celestial temper, to do battle against Abaddon.

Nor will he be silenced; talking terribly against all talking but his own; agreeing, disagreeing, all the same, he the Jove permitting none, none, to mount Olympus till the god deign silence and invite. Curious to see him monologizing, his chin aloft, the pent thunders rolling, lightnings darting from under his bold brows, words that tell of the wail within, accents not meant for music, yet made lyrical in the cadences of his Caledonian refrain, his mirth mad as Lear's, his humor wilful as the winds. Not himself then is approachable by himself even.

A lovable man, nevertheless, with a great heart in his

breast, sympathies the kindliest, deepest, nor indifferent
to the ills the flesh is heir to. Why, oh ye powers, this
wretchedness amidst the means superabounding for re-
lieving and preventing it? Why this taking up reform
forever from the beggar and felon side, as if these were
sole credentials to sympathy, essential elements of the
social state? Rather let force, persistent yet beneficent,
be brought to bear upon mankind, giving alike to prince
and people the dutiful drill that alone equips for the
tasks of life, — this were the State's duty, the province
of rulers; a thing to set about at once with the vigor
of righteousness that justice demands for the rule of
the world.

The way of Imperialism this, and playing Providence
harshly. He mistakes in commending absoluteism to republicans, especially in times like ours. England, even,
imperial as she is, is too intelligent and free to accept it.
America certainly cannot. If he would but believe in
the people, divide his faith in hero-worship with masses,
also. But it is not easy for a Briton to comprehend
properly republican institutions like ours. Nothing
short of success against large odds can convince him
of the feasibility, the safety of a popular government.

> " Success, success; to thee, to thee,
>   As to a god, he bends the knee."

Not one of his heroes would serve our turn. Frederick were perhaps a fit captain to dominate over a
brute multitude; Cromwell might serve in a state of

revolution, but must fail altogether at reconstruction. Even Milton, the republican, would hardly avail with' republicans freed from the old British love of sway.

It is not safe for any to dwell long on Sinai, leaving the multitudes meanwhile to their idolatries below. In rigors thus austere the humanities perish. Justice and mercy must alike conspire in the fulfiment of the decalogue, lest vengeance break the tables and shatter the divine image also.

"When heaven would save a man, it encircles him with compassion."

JULY.

"O tenderly the haughty day
  Fills his blue urn with fire;
 One morn is in the mighty heaven,
   And one in our desire."

— *Emerson.*

INDEPENDENCE DAY.

A ND the republic now begins to look sweet and
beautiful again, as if men and patriotic citizens
might walk upright without shame or apologies of any
sort. Having managed for a century or more to keep
the black man under foot, provoked a war to this end,
and, in our straits, availed of his life to spare ours, let
us cherish the faith that we are bent honestly now on
securing him the rights which his courage and loyalty
have won for him and his while the republic stands.
Was this slaughter of men and expenditure of treasure,
with the possible woes to come, necessary to make us
just? And shall we not be careful hereafter that political parties play not false as before the war ; the cry
for union and reconstruction but a specious phrase for
reinstating the old issues under new names? Admitted
into the Union, the once rebellious States may break
out into new atrocities for recovering their fallen fortunes. It behooves the friends of freedom and human
rights to know their friends, and trust those, and only

those, who have proved themselves faithful in the dire struggle, —

> "Who faithful in insane sedition keep,
> With silver and with ruddy gold may vie."

In democratic times like ours, when Power is stealing the world over from the few to the many, and with an impetus unprecedented in the world's history, the rightful depositories of Power, the People, should make sure that their representatives are fitted alike and disposed to administer affairs honorably; the rule being that of the Best by the Best, — an aristocracy in essence as in name; since no calamity can befall a people like the want of good heads to give it stability and self-respect in its own, or consideration in the eyes of foreign beholders. Ideas are the royal Presidents; States and peoples intelligent and prosperous as they are loyal to these Potentates. Liberty is the highest of trusts committed to man by his Creator, and in the enjoyment of which man becomes himself a creator, — a trust at once the most sacred and most difficult to hold inviolate. "Power is a fillet that presses so hard the temples that few can take it up safely." Right is the royal ruler alone, and he who rules with least restraint comes nearest to empire.

And one of the most hopeful aspects of our national affairs is the coming into importance and power of plain, sensible men, like Grant and Boutwell, — men owing their places to their honesty and useful services,

— the one in the field, the other in the state. Our village, also, is honored by the elevation of one of its distinguished citizens for his eminent legal attainments and personal integrity. This change for the better in our politics, it seems, came in with President Lincoln, himself the plainest of the plain, one of the most American of American men ; is (after his successor's lamentable career) now reinstated in our present chief magistrate, whose popularity is scarcely secondary to any of his predecessors in the Presidential Chair. Our national politics have obviously improved in these respects upon later administrations, and we may reasonably hope for the prevalence of peace and prosperity, such as the country has not enjoyed since the times of Washington and Franklin. The reign of principle appears to have returned into the administration of affairs, honorable men taking the lead, softening, in large measure, the asperities and feuds of parties. Great questions affecting the welfare of the community, and for the solution of which the ablest heads are requisite, are coming into discussion, and are to be settled for the benefit, we trust, of all concerned. Reform in capital and labor, temperance, woman's social and political condition, popular education, powers of corporations, international communication, — these and the new issues which their settlement will effect, must interest and occupy the active forces of the country to plant the republic, upon stable foundations.

8

"An early, good education," says Gray, in his notes on Plato's Republic, "is the best means of turning the eyes of the mind from the darkness and uncertainty of popular opinion, to the clear light of truth. It is the interest of the public neither to suffer unlettered and unphilosophical minds to meddle with government, nor to allow men of knowledge to give themselves up for the whole of life to contemplation; as the first will lack principle to guide them, and others want practice and inclination to business." One might also commend to senators and representatives this sentence from Tacitus: "I speak," he says, "of popular eloquence, the genuine offspring of that licentiousness to which fools and designing men have given the name of liberty. I speak of that bold and turbulent oratory, that inflamer of the people, and constant companion of sedition, that fierce incendiary that knows no compliance, and scorns to temporize, — busy, rash, and arrogant, but, in quiet and well-regulated governments, utterly unknown." Yet I cannot say that I should have written, with my present notion of political or religious obligation, what follows: "Upon the whole, since no man can enjoy a state of calm tranquillity, and, at the same time, raise a great and splendid reputation; to be content with the benefits of the age in which we live, without detracting from our ancestors, is the virtue that best becomes us." The sentiment has a patriotic sound, but conceals the cardinal truth, dear to a patriot, certainly in our times and republic, that a calm tranquillity is hardly compatible with a life of heroic action, and that true progress, so far from detracting from the glory of our ancestors, carries forward that for which they battled and bled, to clothe them and their descendants with a fresher and more enduring fame. Not in imitation of such inflamers of the people, but in the spirit of liberty and loyalty, have Sumner and Phillips won great and splendid reputations, if not silenced the fools and designing men whose bold and turbulent oratory, the genuine offspring of licentiousness, once sounded in our national halls, and came near the separation of our Union.

Whom did the people trust?
Not those, the false confederates of State,
Who laid their country's fortunes desolate;
Plucked her fair ensigns down to seal the black man's fate;
Not these secured their trust.

But they, the generous and the just,
Who, nobly free and truly great,
Served steadfast still the servant race
As masters in the menial's place;
By their dark brothers strove to stand
Till owners these of mind and hand,
And freedom's banners waved o'er an enfranchised land.

These were the nation's trust, —
The patriots brave and just.

PHILLIPS.

" Some men such rare parts have that they can swim
   If favor nor occasion help not them."

Phillips stands conspicuous above most of his time,
as the advocate of human rights, the defender óf the
oppressed.   By happy fortune, he enjoys the privilege
denied to senators, of speaking unencumbered by con-
vention or caucus.   His speeches have the highest
qualities of an orator.   In range of thought, clearness
of statement, keen satire, brilliant wit, personal anecdote, wholesome moral sentiment, the Puritan spirit,
they are unmatched by any of the great orators of his
time.   They have, besides, the rare merit, and one in
which our public men have been painfully deficient, of
straightforwardness and truth to the hour.   They are
addressed to the conscience of the country, are spoken
in the interest of humanity.   Many a soldier in the
field during the late war, many a citizen owes his loyalty to hearing his eloquent words.

Above party, unless it be the honorable and ancient
party of mankind, they embody the temper and drift of
the times.   How many public men are here to survive
in the pillory of his indignant invectives !   The history
of the last thirty years cannot be accurately written
without his facts and anecdotes.   There is no great interest of philanthropy in which he has not been, and
still is, active.   His words are to be taken as those of
an earnest mind intent on furthering the ends of justice,

interpreted not by their rhetoric, but strict adherence to principle. Certainly the country has at times hung in the balance of his argument; cabinets and councils hesitating to do or undo without some regard to his words, well knowing the better constituency which he better represents and speaks for, — the people, namely, whose breath can unmake as it has made.

An earnest, truthful man, he has not shared with other statesmen of his time in their indifferency nor their despair; and if by some esteemed a demagogue and disorganizer, such is not his estimate of the part taken by him in the great issues of the past, political and social. The friend of progress, he early threw himself into the conflict, addressed himself to the issues as they rose, rose with them and rode the wave bravely; sometimes hastening, oftentimes provoking the crisis. What States would not adventure upon as policy, he espoused as policy and humanity both. Addressing himself from the first to the great middle class, whose principles are less corrupted by party politics, in whom the free destiny of peoples is lodged, he is gathering the elements of power and authority which, becoming formidable in ability if not in numbers, must secure the country's confidence, and in due time have political dictation and rule.

Then, of the new instrumentalities for agitation and reform, the free Platform derives largely its popularity and efficiency from his genius. Consider the freedom of speech it invites and maintains, free as the freest can make it, a stand whereon every one who will gains a hearing ; every opinion its widest scope of entertainment, — the widest hospitality consistent with the decorum of debate.   Hither comes any one breathing a sentiment of progress, any daring to dissent against dissent, against progress itself.   Here the sexes meet on fair terms. Here, as not elsewhere, is intimated, if not spoken fittingly, the popular spirit and tendency.   Here come the most effective speakers by preference to address a free constituency, a constituency to be theirs, if not already, their words leaping into type from their lips, to be spread forthwith to the four winds by the reporting press.   'T is a school of debate, for oratory, for thought, for practice ; has the remarkable merit of freshness, originality ; questions affecting the public welfare being here anticipated, first deliberated upon by the people themselves ; systems of agitation organized and set on foot for creating a wholesome popular sentiment ; in short, for giving inspiration, a culture, to the country, which the universities cannot ; training the reason and moral sense by direct dealing with principles and persons as occasion requires ; a school from whence have graduated not a few of our popular speakers, — the Orator himself, whose speeches furnish passages for collegiate declamation, from which politicians plume their rhetoric to win a borrowed fame. Cato said, " An orator was a good man skilled in the art of speaking."

More than any lecturer, unless it be Emerson, he has

made the lecture a New-England, if not an American institution; is always heard with profit and pleasure by the unprejudiced auditor, — any course in the cities and towns being thought incomplete without his. Nor is it easy to estimate the debt of the free States to his speeches before associations, conventions, in pulpits, the humblest places where his words could be secured. He has already taken his place beside Garrison, has linked his name with the Liberator's, to be on men's lips while the word *slave* has significance.

If there be any one to whom the country is more largely indebted than another for eminent services in his day, it must be Garrison; unless a doubt may arise in the minds of some, if the hero of Harper's Ferry be not entitled to like honors, since to these illustrious men must be attributed the merit of having struck the most effective blows for the overthrow of slavery, the one inaugurating the era of emancipation, and the other consummating it.

> "The just man's like a rock, that turns the wroth
> Of all the raging waters into a froth."

The agitation and outside pressure which they were chiefly instrumental in furthering to its rightful issues, were the most powerful auxiliaries, if not the power itself, which emancipated the mind of the country from its subserviency to the slave dominion. They were the creators of the sentiment that freed the negro at last from his bonds and cleared the way for a true Republican State. Some power superior to the Constitution was required to revise it, and free the whole people from this Arachne's coil that had bound them so long; was especially needed to extricate the rulers themselves from its meshes, and to rescue the rights thus imperilled by unscrupulous placemen who shrunk from the task. These could not help them, caught in the same snare that bound the nation. "Neither the law, nor the Constitution, nor the whole system of American institutions," they were told, "ever had contemplated a case as likely to arise under our system in which a resort would be necessary to provide outside of the law and Constitution for amending the Constitution." The case arose, nevertheless, and was provided for by these powerful agitators, and by the progress of events. The late civil outbreak compelled the necessary amendments, sweeping the compromises, the slave Congress and territory from the statute books and the country itself.

> "Principles like fountains flow round forever,
>   Being in a state of perpetual agitation."

"To all new truths, all renovations of old truths," says Coleridge, "it must be as in the ark between the destroyed and the about-to-be-renovated world. The raven must be sent out before the dove, and ominous controversy must precede peace and the olive wreath."

GREELEY.

Of political editors, next to Garrison, perhaps Horace Greeley was the most efficient in furthering this national result; and by his eminent services in various departments of activity comes nearest to being the people's man, the best representative of character indigenous to New England, or more properly America — like Beecher and Phillips. His power appears to lie in his strong understanding, abundant information, plain statement of his facts, freed from all rhetorical embellishment. A rustic Franklin in his direct way of putting his things before his auditor, he makes plain his meaning in spite of his utter want of all graces of person, or of oratory, handling his subject as a rude farmer his axe and crowbar. There is about him a homely charm of good-nature, a child-like candor, that have all the effect of eloquence, elevating him for the time into the subject he treats. In the statistics of things, practical and political, he is a kind of living encyclopedia of information, and as his chief distinction has made the newspaper a power it had not been before.

May we not credit New England with giving the country these new Instrumentalities for Progress, viz. : —

> Greeley, the Newspaper ;
> Garrison, a free Platform ;
> Phillips, a free Convention ;
> Beecher, a free Pulpit ;
> Emerson, the Lecture ?

The Conversation awaits being added to the list.

AGE OF IRON AND BRONZE.

FRIDAY, **9.**

OURS can hardly claim to be the Golden Age, but of Bronze and Iron rather. If ideas are in the ascendant, still mind is fettered by mechanism. We scale the heavens to grade the spaces. Messrs. Capital & Co. transact our business for us the globe over. Was it in the Empire News that I read the company's advertisement for supplying mankind with gas at a penny *per diem* annually? And then, proceeding to say, " that considering the old-time monopoly in the heavenly luminary, the corporation has constructed at fabulous cost their Brazen Cope to shut down upon the horizon at day-break punctually, and so graduate to each customer's tube his just allowance, else darkness for delinquents the year round."

Certainly a splendid conception for distributing sun-beams by the Globe Corporation if the solar partner consent to the speculation. Had Hesiod the enterprise in mind when he sung, —

" Seek virtue first, and after virtue, coin "?

Or St. Paul, when writing concerning labor and cap-ital : " For I would not," he says, " that other men should be eased and you burdened, but by an equality that now at the time your abundance may be a supply for their want, that their abundance may also be a supply for your want, that there may be an equality, as it is written, He that had gathered much, had nothing over, and he that had gathered little, had no lack. If any man will not work, neither should he eat."

Any attempt to simplify and supply one's wants by abstinence and self-help is in the most hopeful direction, and serviceable to the individual whether his experiment succeed or not, the practice of most, from the beginning, having been to multiply rather than diminish one's natural wants, and thus to become poor at the cost of becoming rich. "Who has the fewest wants," said Socrates, " is most like God."

"Who wishes, wants, and whoso wants is poor."

Our " Fruitlands " was an adventure undertaken in good faith for planting a Family Order here in New England, in hopes of enjoying a pastoral life with a few devoted men and women, smitten with sentiments of the old heroism and love of holiness and of humanity. But none of us were prepared to actualize practically the ideal life of which we dreamed. So we fell apart, some returning to the established ways, some soured by the trial, others postponing the fulfilment of his dream to a more propitious future.*

---

* "FRUITLANDS.

" We have received a communication from Messrs. Alcott and Lane, dated from their farm, *Fruitlands*, in Harvard, Massachusetts, from which we make the following extract: —

" ' We have made an arrangement with the proprietor of an estate of about a hundred acres, which liberates this tract from human ownership. For

I certainly esteem it an inestimable privilege to have been bred to outdoor labors, the use of tools, and to find myself the owner of a garden, with the advantage of laboring sometimes besides my faithful Irishman, and compare views of men and things with him. I think myself the greater gainer of the two by this intercourse. Unbiassed by books, and looking at things as they stand related to his senses and simple needs, I learn naturally what otherwise I should not have known so well, if at all. The sympathy and sincerity are the best part of it. One sees the more clearly his social relations and duties; sees the need of

---

picturesque beauty, both in the near and the distant landscape, the spot has few rivals. A semicircle of undulating hills stretches from south to west, among which the Wachusett and Monadnock are conspicuous. The vale, through which flows a tributary to the Nashua, is esteemed for its fertility and ease of cultivation, is adorned with groves of nut trees, maples, and pines, and watered by small streams. Distant not thirty miles from the metropolis of New England, this reserve lies in a serene and sequestered dell. No public thoroughfare invades it, but it is entered by a private road. The nearest hamlet is that of Stillriver, a field's walk of twenty minutes, and the village of Harvard is reached by circuitous and hilly roads of nearly three miles.

" ' Here we prosecute our effort to initiate a Family in harmony with the primitive instincts in man. The present buildings being ill placed and unsightly as well as inconvenient, are to be temporarily used, until suitable and tasteful buildings in harmony with the natural scene can be completed. An excellent site offers itself on the skirts of the nearest wood, affording shade and shelter, and commanding a view of the lands of the estate, nearly all of which are capable of spade culture. It is intended to adorn the pastures with orchards, and to supersede ultimately the labor of the plough and cattle, by the spade and the pruning-knife.

" ' Our planting and other works, both without and within doors, are already in active progress. The present Family numbers ten individuals, five

beneficent reforms in the economics of labor and capital
by which the working classes shall have their just claims
allowed, the products of hand and brain be more equit-
ably distributed, a finer sympathy and wiser humanity
prevail in the disposition of affairs. No true man can
be indifferent to that great productive multitude, without whose industry capitalists would have nothing in
which to invest; the callings and the professions lack
bread and occupation alike. Head and hands best
co-operate in this interplay of services. Every gift, besides enriching its owner, should enrich the whole community, opportunities be opened for the free exercise

being children of the founders. Ordinary secular farming is not our object.
Fruit, grain, pulse, garden plants and herbs, flax and other vegetable products for food, raiment, and domestic uses, receiving assiduous attention,
afford at once ample manual occupation, and chaste supplies for the bodily
needs. Consecrated to human freedom, the land awaits the sober culture of
devout men.

" ' Beginning with small pecuniary means, this enterprise must be rooted
in a reliance on the succors of an ever-bounteous Providence, whose vital
affinities being secured by this union with uncorrupted fields and unworldly
persons, the cares and injuries of a life of gain are avoided.

" ' The inner nature of every member of the Family is at no time neglected. A constant leaning on the living spirit within the soul should conse-
crate every talent to holy uses, cherishing the widest charities. The choice
Library (of which a partial catalogue was given in Dial No. XII) is accessible to all who are desirous of perusing these records of piety and wisdom.
Our plan contemplates all such disciplines, cultures, and habits as evidently
conduce to the purifying and edifying of the inmates. Pledged to the Spirit
alone, the founders can anticipate no hasty or numerous accession to their
numbers. The kingdom of peace is entered only through the gates of self-
denial and abandonment; and blessedness is the test and the reward of
obedience to the unswerving law of Love.— *The Dial.*

" ' JUNE 10, 1843.' "

of all, the golden rule stand for something besides an idle text. Every one is entitled to a competence, provided he employs his gifts for the common good. It seems but right that the gifted should return to the common treasury in the ratio of their endowments; be taxed at a higher rate than those to whom like advantages have been denied. Indeed, it is questionable whether the man who is poor by no fault of his, should be taxed at all; give him citizenship rather as an inborn right, as a man, not as a mere producer. Men are loyal from other considerations than self-interest. One would not check the spirit of accumulation, but the monopoly of the gift for the sole benefit of the oppressor. A competence, including every comfort, and even harmless luxuries, is what all men need, all desire, all might have, were there a fair distribution of the avails of labor, opportunities for labor of head or hand for all, — the right to be educated and virtuous included, as the most important. The poor man cannot compete, practically, successfully, with the rich man, the laborer with the capitalist, the ignorant with the instructed, — all are placed at unequal odds, the victims of circumstances which they did not create, and which those who do may use to their injury if they choose. The laborer is broken on the wheel his necessities compel him to drive, feeling the while the wrong done him by those whom he has enriched by his toil.

No tradition assigns a beginning to justice, but only to injustice. Before the Silver, the Brazen, the Iron, comes the Golden Age, when virtue is current, and man at his highest value. It is when man is degraded that virtue and justice are dishonored, and labor deemed disreputable.

Poverty may be the philosopher's ornament. Too rich to need, and self-respecting to receive benefits, save upon terms which render the receiver the nobler giver, he revenges upon fortune by possessing a kingdom superior to mischance and incumbrance.

> The gold alone but gold can buy,
> Wisdom's the sterling currency.

CONVERSATION ON ENTHUSIASM.*

WEDNESDAY, 14.

MR. ALCOTT began the conversation by referring to that of Monday before, on the subject of Temperament and Complexion, and added other fine thoughts about it.

He said, perhaps he had dwelt too much on the symbol of color, but conceived himself borne out in all he had said. "The Greeks held that a brown complexion betokened courage, and those who had fair skins were called children of light and favorites of the gods. And the gods themselves were demonic or divine, as tempered by darkness or light, — the gods Infernal, the

---

* Printed from notes taken by a lady (Miss Ariana Walker) at the time. The conversation was held in Boston in December, 1849.

Midgods, the Celestials. So Christian art has painted Satan dark, the Christ fair. And late experiments on the sunbeam showed that dark substances imprison the rays, — these absorbing more and delivering less. The more of sun, so much the more of soul; the less of sun, of passion more, and the strange fire. He fancied black eyes were of Oriental descent, were tinged less or more with fairer hues in crossing West. People of sandy hair and florid complexions were of Northern ancestry. The fusion of the various races was now taking place, blending all, doubtless, into a more harmonious and beautiful type.

He asked if there did not lurk in the fancy, if not in our atoms, a persuasion that complexion, like features, voice, gait, typified and emblazoned personal traits of their possessors, if the rhetoric of morals and religion did not revel in like distinctions. " Handsome is that handsome does." Beauty was the birthright of all, if not their inheritance. It was shame that brought deformity into the world. Every child accused, he knew not whom, for any blemish of his. " Why not mine the happy star, too?" Still some trait was insinuated into the least favored, and stamped upon the embryonic clay. Ebony, alabaster, indigo, vermillion, the pigments were all mingled as purity or passion decreed. Types were persistent, family features standing strong for centuries and perpetuating themselves from generation to generation. Place the portraits of a long line of ancestors on the walls, one's features were

all there, with the slight variations arising from inter-
marriage, degrees of culture, calling, climate.

"Our faces were our coats of arms."

"Eyes were most characteristic. These played the
prime parts in life, — eyes and voice. Eyes were a
civility and a kingdom: voice a fortune. There was a
culture, a fate in them, direful, divine." And he
quoted, without naming the author: —

> "Black eyes, in your dark orbs doth lie
> My ill or happy destiny;
> If with clear looks you me behold,
> You give me wine and mounts of gold;
> If you dart forth disdainful rays,
> To your own dye you turn my days;
> Black eyes, in your dark orbs doth dwell
> My bane or bliss, my heaven or hell."

Then added, significantly: —

> Ask you *my* preference, what their hue?
> Surely the safe, celestial blue.

He said: "Voice classified us. The harmonious
voice tells of the harmonious soul. Millions of fiends
are evoked in a breath by an irritated one. A gentle
voice converts the Furies into Muses. The highest
saint is not he who strives the most violently, but he
upon whom goodness sits gracefully, whose strength is
gentleness, duty loved, because spontaneous, and who
wastes none of his power in effort; his will being one
and above temptation. True love says, ' Come to my

embrace, you are safer with me than you were with yourself, since I am wise above knowledge, and tasting of the apple.' The sequel is bliss and peace. But after fascination comes sorrow, remorse. The touch of the demonized soul is poison. Read Swedenborg's Hells, he added, and beware of demonized eyes ! "

I never saw any one who seemed to purify words as Mr. Alcott does; with him nothing is common or unclean.

He then spoke of temperance in its widest sense, as being that which contributed to health of the whole being, body and soul alike. He said, " We should breakfast on sunrise and sup on sunset." And he read passages from Pythagoras, recommending music as a diet. Pythagoras composed melodies for the night and morning, to purify the brain. He forbade his disciples the using of flesh meats, or drinks which heated and disturbed the brain, or hindered the music of dreams."

At this point of the conversation, Miss Bremer and Mr. Benzon, the Swedish consul, came in, and there was a slight pause.

Mr. Alcott then resumed the subject, and read Emerson's Bacchus, to which he gave new significance. When he had finished, he said, " This is the wine we want." He then spoke of the subject proposed for the evening's conversation, which was Enthusiasm, defining it as " an abandonment to the instincts. The seer," he said, " was one in whom memory predominated, and many of his visions were recollections rather of a former than revelations of a future state." This state of clairvoyance he named " thought a-bed, or philosophy recumbent " ; and in this view he spoke of " Swedenborg, who was an enthusiast in the latter sense, and revealed remarkable things." He quoted a passage from Swedenborg's diary, wherein he speaks of his being created with the power of breathing inwardly, suspending his outward breathing, and in this way conversed with angels and spirits.

Miss Bremer asked Mr. Alcott " if he called Swedenborg an enthusiast."

Mr. Alcott said, " Swedenborg was in such fine relations with nature and spirit, that many things seemed revealed to him beyond the apprehension of ordinary men. He was a seer rather of supernatural than of spiritual things ; a preternaturalist, rather than spiritualist. He had wonderful insights into nature, also, which science was almost every day confirming."

" His followers claimed that he anticipated important discoveries, both in natural as in spiritual science, and that his merits were enhanced by his claim to supernatural illumination. And whatever his gifts, how assisted, whether by agencies supernatural or preternatural, their operations were of wonderful sweep, his insights surpassing, transcending the comprehension of any successor ; of a kind that have led some to suspect that he staggered down under the weight of his endowments. Certainly, he stands, like Boehme, an exceptional mind, in the order of nature, and awaits an interpreter to determine his place in the world of thought. He is the most eminent example furnished in modern biography of the possibilities of the metempsychosis, as if we saw in him an ability to translate himself at will, personally, wheresoever he would, taking his residence for the while in plant, animal, mineral, atom, with the superadded faculty of ravishing its secret. Nor content with this, he ransacks the primeval elements, the limbos of chaos and night. What burglaries he perpetrates ! picking of locks, slitting of mysteries, opening rents into things sacred and profane, — of these no end. Then such edifices rising from regions of vagary and shadow, a goblin world, grand, grotesque, seldom lighted from above, or tipped with azure. His heavens had no prospects ; no perspective ; his hells were lurid ; the pit bottomless, a Stygian realm throughout. His genius plunges, seldom soars ; is not fledged, but footed ; his heaven but the cope of the abyss in plain sight of the doomed. His angels are spectral, unwholesome ; his celestials too knowing to be innocent.

" It were a fruitless task to follow him from starting-point to goal, if goal there be, in his restless racing throughout nature. The ghost-seer of shadow-land, whereinto he smuggled all natural things as spiritual phantoms ; he needs be studied with due drawback of doubt, as to the veracity of his claim to divine illumination. Still with every abatement, here is a body of truth none can gainsay nor resist ; abysses not yet fathomed by any successor, naturalist, or spiritualist.

After this surprising statement of his views of Swedenborg, Miss Bremer asked more questions about Mr. Alcott's definition of an Enthusiast, adding : " Christ, then, if we speak of him as a man, was an enthusiast."

Mr. Alcott, smiling, said, " Yes, the divinest of enthusiasts, surrendering himself entirely to the instincts of the Spirit ; might safely do so, being holy, whole, inspired throughout all his gifts, his whole Personality, — the divine fire pervaded every part ; therefore he was the celestial man."

The conversation here turned upon Nature, in some way which I do not now recollect, and Mr. Alcott spoke of the great mission of the prophet of nature.

" The public child of earth and sky."

" Nature," he said, " was more to some persons than others ; they standing in closer relations to it."

" But nature," said Miss Bremer, " is not wholly good."

" No," said Mr. Alcott ; " there is something of Fate in her, too, as in some persons. She, too, is a little bitten."

The expression seemed to amuse her, for she repeated it several times, laughing.

Mr. Alcott then said, " that nature was not wholly sane. It was given to the celestial man alone to take from it only what was salutary, as it was the Nemesis

of the demonic man to take what was hurtful.   Bees
gathered honey from all flowers."

James Russell Lowell asked " if bees did not sometimes secrete poisonous honey? "

Mr. Alcott said " he believed they did, but only when
wholesome flowers were denied them."

Miss Littlehale suggested that " honey was not poisonous to the bees, but to men only, and Mr. Lowell
allowed that it was not."

Miss Bremer now returned to the word Enthusiast.
She said Mr. Alcott had defined it well as " divine
intoxication."

I do not follow the order of time in what follows, but
record some scattered sayings of the conversation.

Mr. Alcott spoke of " the celestial, or unfallen man,
as not making choice of good; he was chosen rather;
elected, deliberation presupposed a mixed will, a temptation and a lapse. Then, opening Plotinus, he read
this beautiful passage : —

" Every soul is a Venus.   And this, the nativity of
Venus, and Love who was born at the same time with
her, obscurely signify. The soul, therefore, when in
a condition conformable to nature, loves God, wishing
to be united to him, being, as it were, the desire of
a beautiful virgin to be conjoined with a beautiful
love.   When, however, the soul descends into generation, then being, as it were, deceived by spurious
nuptials, and associating herself with another and mortal love, she becomes petulent and insolent, through

being absent from her father. But when she again hates wantonness and injustice, and becomes purified from the defilements which are here, and again returns to her father, she is affected in the most felicitous manner. And those, indeed, who are ignorant of this affection, may from worldly love form some conjecture of divine love, by considering how great a felicity the possession of a most beloved object is conceived to be; and also, by considering that those earthly objects of love are mortal and noxious; that the love of them is nothing more than the love of images, and that they lose their attractive power because they are not truly desirable, nor our real good, nor that which we investigate. In the ideal world, however, the object of love is to be found, with which we may be conjoined, which we may participate and truly possess, and which is not externally enveloped with flesh. He, however, who knows this, well knew what I say, and will be convinced that the soul has another life."

Miss Bremer seemed puzzled by this reading as questioning in her mind a distinction between virtue and innocence, or holiness, which Mr. Alcott had discriminated clearly.

Some one inquired, "How can we trust our instincts since these have been so differently educated?"

Mr. Alcott said "they had rather been overborne by the appetites and passions. It was the tragedy of life that these were obscured so soon, and the mind left in confusion. The child was more of an enthusiast than the man ordinarily. And then so many were born old;

even in the babe one sometimes sees some ancient sinner. Youth is so attractive because still under the sway of instinct. The highest duty is musical and sings itself. Business, lusts, draw men downwards. Yet were life earnest and true to the instincts, it would be music and song. Life was too much for most. No one was always an enthusiast. It was in the golden moments that he was filled with the overflowing divinity. The blissful moments were those when one abandons himself to the Spirit, letting it do what it will with him. True, most persons were divided, there were two or more of them, — a Deuce distracting them and they in conflict with evils, or devils. But what is the bad but lapse from the good, — the good blindfolded?"

"Ah! Mr. Alcott," said Miss Bremer, laughing, "I am desperately afraid there is a little bit of a devil, after all."

"One's foes are of his own household," said **Mr. Alcott.** "If his house is haunted it is by himself only." Our Choices were our Saviours or Satans.

Speaking of the temperaments, Mr. Alcott discriminated these in their different elements.

The celestial man was composed more largely of light and ether. The demonic man combined more of fire and vapor. The animal man more of embers and dust.*

---

* THE TEMPERAMENTS AND COMPLEXIONS.
    The Sanguine or Aeriform is Fair;
    The Choleric or Fiery is Florid;
    The Lymphatic or Aqueous is Olive;
    The Melancholic or Earthy is Dark.
  The four are mostly blended in life, the fusion being frequently indeterminable.

The sacraments might be considered symbolically, as Baptism, or purification by water.

Fasting, or temperance in outward delights.

Continence, or chastity in personal indulgences.

Prayer, or aspiring aims.

Labor, or prayer in act or pursuits.

These he considered the regimen of inspiration and thought.

Mr. Alcott closed the conversation by reading from the Paradise Regained a description of the banquet spread by Satan for Christ; also, the lines in praise of Chastity, from the Comus, whose clear statue-like beauty always affects one powerfully.

HAWTHORNE.

MONDAY, 19.

HAWTHORNE was of the darker temperament and tendencies. His sensitiveness and sadness were native, and he cultivated them apparently alike by solitude, the pursuits and studies in which he indulged, till he became almost fated to know gayer hours only by stealth. By disposition friendly, he seemed the victim of his temperament, as if he sought distance, if not his pen, to put himself in communication, and possible sympathy with others,—with his nearest friends, even. His reserve and imprisonment were more distant and close, while the desire for conversation was livelier, than any one I have known. There was something of strangeness even

9

in his cherished intimacies, as if he set himself afar from all and from himself with the rest; the most diffident of men, as coy as a maiden, he could only be won by some cunning artifice, his reserve was so habitual, his isolation so entire, the solitude so vast. How distant people were from him, the world they lived in, how he came to know so much about them, by what stratagem he got into his own house or left it, was a marvel. Fancy fixed, he was not to be jostled from himself for a moment, his mood was so persistent. There he was in the twilight, there he stayed. Was he some damsel imprisoned in that manly form pleading alway for release, sighing for the freedom and companionships denied her? Or was he some Assyrian ill at ease afar from the olives and the East? Had he strayed over with William the Conqueror, and true to his Norman nature, was the baron still in republican America, secure in his castle, secure in his tower, whence he could defy all invasion of curious eyes? What neighbor of his ever caught him on the highway, or ventured to approach his threshold?

> " His bolted Castle gates, what man should ope,
>   Unless the Lord did will
>   To prove his skill,
> And tempt the fates hid in his horoscope?"

Yet if by chance admitted, welcome in a voice that a woman might own for its hesitancy and tenderness; his eyes telling the rest.

> " For such the noble language of his eye,
>   That when of words his lips were destitute,
>   Kind eyebeams spake while yet his tongue was mute."

Your intrusion was worth the courage it cost; it emboldened to future assaults to carry this fort of bashfulness. During all the time he lived near me, our estates being separated only by a gate and shaded avenue, I seldom caught sight of him; and when I did it was but to lose it the moment he suspected he was visible; oftenest seen on his hill-top screened behind the shrubbery and disappearing like a hare into the bush when surprised. I remember of his being in my house but twice, and then he was so ill at ease that he found excuse for leaving politely forthwith, — "the stove was so hot," "the clock ticked so loud." Yet he once complained to me of his wish to meet oftener, and dwelt on the delights of fellowship, regretting he had so little. I think he seldom dined from home; nor did he often entertain any one, — once, an Englishman, when I was also his guest; but he preserved his shrinking taciturnity, and left to us the conversation. Another time I dined with a Southern guest at his table. The conversation turning on the war after dinner, he hid himself in the corner, as if a distant spectator, and fearing there was danger even there. It was due to his guest to hear the human side of the question of slavery, since she had heard only the best the South had to plead in its favor.

I never deemed Hawthorne an advocate of Southern ideas and institutions. He professed democracy, not in the party, but large sense of equality. Perhaps he loved England too well to be quite just to his native land, —

was more the Old Englishman than the New. He seemed to regret the transplanting, as if reluctant to fix his roots in our soil. His book on England, entitled "Our Old Home," intimates his filial affection for that and its institutions. If his themes were American, his treatment of them was foreign, rather. He stood apart as having no stake in home affairs. While calling himself a democrat, he sympathized apparently with the absolutism of the old countries. He had not full faith in the people; perhaps feared republicanism because it had. Of our literary men, he least sympathized with the North, and was tremulously disturbed, I remember, at the time of the New-York mob. It is doubtful if he ever attended a political meeting or voted on any occasion throughout the long struggle with slavery. He stood aloof, hesitating to take a responsible part, true to his convictions, doubtless, strictly honest, if not patriotic.

He strove by disposition to be sunny and genial, traits not native to him. Constitutionally shy, recluse, melancholy, only by shafts of wit and flow of humor could he deliver himself. There was a soft sadness in his smile, a reserve in his glance, telling how isolate he was. Was he ever one of his company while in it? There was an aloofness, a *besides*, that refused to affiliate himself with himself, even. His readers must feel this, while unable to account for it, perhaps, or express it adequately. A believer in transmitted traits needs but read his pedigree to find the genesis of what characterized him distinctly, and made him and his writings their inevitable sequel. Everywhere you will find persons of his type and complexion similar in cast of character and opinions. His associates mostly confirm the observation.

LANDOR.

Landor's Biography, edited by James Forster, and lately published here, well repays perusal. Landor seems to have been the victim of his temperament all his life long. I know not when I have read a commentary so appalling on the fate that breaks a noble mind on the wheel of its passions, precipitating it into the dungeons but to brighten its lights. Of impetuous wing, his genius was yet sure of its boldest flights, and to him, if any modern, may be applied Coleridge's epithet of " myriad mindedness," so salient, varied, so daring the sweep of his thought. More than any he reminds of Shakespeare in dramatic power ; of Plato, in his mastery of dialogue ; in epic force, of Æschylus. He seems to have been one of the demigods, cast down, out of place, out of his time, restless ever, and indignant at his destiny, —

" Heaven's exile straying from the orb of light."

His stormful, wayward career exemplifies in a remarkable manner the recoiling Fate pervading human affairs.

" A sharp dogmatic man," says Emerson, who met him when abroad, " with a great deal of knowledge, a great deal of worth and a great deal of pride, with a profound contempt for all that he does not understand, a master of elegant learning and capable of the utmost delicacy of sentiment, and yet prone to indulge a sort of ostentation of coarse imagery and language. He has capital enough to have furnished the brain of fifty stock authors, yet has written no good book. In these busy days of avarice and ambition, when there is so little disposition to profound thought, or to any but the most superficial intellectual entertainments, a faithful scholar, receiving from past ages the treasures of wit, and enlarging them by his own lore, is a friend and consoler of mankind. Whoever writes for the love of mirth and beauty, and not with ulterior ends, belongs to this sacred class, and among these, few men of the present age have a better claim to be numbered than Mr. Landor. Wherever genius and taste have existed, wherever freedom and justice are threatened (which he values as the element in which genius may work), his interest is here to be commanded. Nay, when we remember his rich and ample page, wherein we are always sure to find free and sustained thought, a keen and precise understanding, an affluent and ready memory familiar with all chosen books, an industrious observation in every department of life, an experience to which nothing has occurred in vain, honor for every just sentiment, and a scourge like that of the Furies for every oppressor, whether public or private, we feel how dignified is this perpetual censor in his cerule chair, and we wish to thank a benefactor of the reading world."

No writer of our time in the difficult species of composition, the dialogue, has attained a success upon so high a plane as Landor in his Conversations, wherein he has treated almost every human interest, brought his characters together, like Plato's interlocutors, from different ages and of differing opinions, using these as representatives of the world's best literature. And besides these his masterpieces, his verses have the chaste and exquisite quality of the best Greek poetry.

" His dialogues number," says his biographer, " not fewer than a hundred and fifty. Different as these were in themselves, it was not the less the distinguishing mark of their genius to be, both in their conformation and in their mass, almost strangely alike ; and it is this unity in their astonishing variety, the fire of an inexpressible genius running through the whole, that gives to his books containing them their place among the books not likely to pass away ; there is scarcely a form or function of the human mind, sincere or sprightly, cogitative or imaginative, historical, fanciful, or real, which has not been exercised or brought into play in this extraordinary series of writings. The world, past and present, is reproduced in them, with its variety and uniformity, its continuity and change."

What Landor says of written dialogue, holds in still wider latitude, even, in conversation.

"When a man writes a dialogue, he has it all to himself, the pro and the con, the argument and the reply. Within the shortest given space of time, he may indulge in every possible variety of mood. He may contradict himself every minute. In the same page, without any sort of violence, the most different shades of sentiment may find expression. Extravagance of statement, which in other forms could not be admitted, may be fully put forth. Dogmas of every description may be dealt in, audaciously propounded, or passionately opposed, with a result all the livelier in proportion to the mere vehemence expended on them. In no other style of composition is a writer so free from ordinary restraints upon opinion, or so absolved from self-control. Better far than any other, it adapts itself to eagerness and impatience. Dispensing with preliminaries, the jump *in medias res* may at once be taken safely. That one thing should be unexpectedly laid aside, and another as capriciously taken up, is quite natural to it; the subjects being few that may not permissively branch off into all the kindred topics connected with them, when the formalities held ordinarily necessary in the higher order of prose composition have disappeared in the freedom of conversation."

SLEEP AND DREAMS.

"When sleep hath closed our eyes the mind sees well,
For Fate by daylight is invisible."

THINGS admirable for the admirable hours. The morning for thought, the afternoon for recreation, the evening for company, the night for rest. Having drank of immortality all night, the genius enters eagerly upon the day's task, impatient of any impertinences jogging the full glass. The best comes when we are at our best; and who so buoyant as to be always rider of the wave? Sleep, and see; wake, and report the nocturnal spectacle. Sleep, like travel, enriches, refreshes, by varying the day's perspective, showing us the night side of the globe we traverse day by day. We make transits too swift for our wakeful senses to follow; pass from solar to lunar consciousness in a twinkling, lapse from forehead and face to occupy our lower parts, and recover, as far as permitted, the keys of genesis and of the foreworlds. "All truth," says Porphyry, "is latent; but this the soul sometimes beholds when she is a little liberated by sleep from the employments of the body. And sometimes she extends her sight, but never perfectly reaches the objects of her vision. Hence, when she beholds, she does not see it with a free and direct light, but through an intervening veil, which the folds of darkening nature draw over her eye. This veil, when in sleep it admits the light to extend as far as truth, is said to be of horn, whose nature is such, from its tenuity, that it is pervious to the light. But when it dulls the sight and repels its vision of truth, it is said to be of ivory, which is a body so naturally dense, that, however thin it may be scraped, it cannot be penetrated by the visual rays."

Homer says, —

"Our dreams descend from Jove."

That is, from the seat of intellect, and declare their import when our will sleeps. Then are they of weighty and reliable import, yet require the like suppression of our will to make plain their significance. Only so is the oracle made reliable. The good alone dream divinely. Our dreams are characteristic of our waking thoughts and states; we are never out of character; never quite another, even when fancy seeks to metamorphose us entirely. The Person is One in all the manifold phases of the Many through which we transmigrate, and we find ourself perpetually, because we cannot lose ourself personally in the mazes of the many. 'T is the one soul in manifold shapes, ever the old friend of the mirror in other face, old and new, yet one in endless revolution and metamorphosis, suggesting a common relationship of forms at their base, with divergent types as these range wider and farther from their central archetype, including all concrete forms in nature, each returning into other, and departing there-from in endless revolution.*

"I catch myself philosophizing most eloquently," wrote Thoreau, "when first returning to consciousnsss in the night or morning. I make the truest observations and distinctions then when the will is yet wholly asleep, and mind works like a machine without friction. I was conscious of having in my sleep transcended the limits of the individual, and made observations and carried on conversations which in my waking hours I can neither recall nor appreciate. As if, in sleep, our individual fell into the infinite mind, and at the moment of awakening we found ourselves on the confines of the latter. On awakening, we resume our enterprise, take up our bodies, and become limited minds again. We meet and converse with those bodies which we have previously animated. There is a moment in the dawn when the darkness of the night is dissipated, and before the exhalations of the day begin to rise, when we see all things more truly than at any other time. The light is more trustworthy, since our senses are pure and the

---

* The seeming miracle and mystery of the mesmeric, or clairvoyant vi-vacity, is best explained by conceiving the instreaming force of the operator driving the magnetic current from cerebrum to the cerebellum of his victim, and there, while under the pressure, reporting the operator's sensations and thoughts through the common brain of both. And this view is confirmed by the further fact that under this dominating force the domain of memory is the more deeply searched, and things revealed which, separate and alone, left unaided by such agencies, neither could have divined. It is like one's adding a double brain to his own, and subsidizing it the while to serve his particular ends.

atmosphere is less gross. By afternoon, all objects are seen in mirage."

All men are spiritualists in finer or coarser manners, as temperament and teaching dictate and determine, — the spiritual world revealing itself accordingly. Speculation has in all ages delighted itself in this preternatural realm from whence have risen the ghosts of realties too unsubstantial and fugitive for ordinary senses to apprehend. Whatever the facts, they receive interpretation according to the spirit and intelligence of the believer. The past is full of such prodigies and phenomena, for whose solution all learning, sacred and profane, is revived in its turn. It appears that like opinions have their rounds to run, like theories with their disciples, reappearing in all great crises of thought, and reaching a fuller solution at each succeeding period. A faith, were such possible, destitute of an element of preternaturalism, or of mysticism, pure or mixed, could not gain general acceptance. Some hold on the invisible connects the known with unknown, yet leaving the copula to be divined. We define it on our lips when we pronounce the word Person, and so approach, as near as we may, to the " I Am " of things.

> Unseen our spirits move, are such,
> So eager they to clasp, they feel, they touch
> While yet our bodies linger, cannot speed
> The distance that divides, confines their need.

GENESIS AND LAPSE.

"BEFORE the Revolution of 1688," says Coleridge, "metaphysics ruled without experimental philosophy. Since the Revolution, experimental psychology has in like manner prevailed, and we now feel the result. In like manner, from Plotinus to Proclus, that is, from A. D. 250 to A. D. 450, philosophy was set up as a substitute for religion; during the dark ages, religion superseded philosophy, and the consequences are equally instructive."

"The great maxim in legislation, intellectual or physical, is *subordinate, not exclude*. Nature, in her ascent, leaves nothing behind; but at each step subordinates and glorifies, — mass, crystal, organ, sensation, sentience, reflection."

Taken in reverse order of descent, Spirit puts itself before, at each step protrudes faculty in feature, function, organ, limb, subordinating to glorify also, — person, volition, thought, sensibility, sense, body, — animating thus and rounding creation to soul and sense alike. The naturalist cannot urge too strongly the claims of physical, nor the plea of the idealist be too vigorously pressed for metaphysical studies. One body in one soul. Nature and spirit are inseparable, and are best studied as a unit. "Either without the other," as Plato said of sex, "is but half itself." Nature ends where spirit begins. The idealist's point of view is the obverse of the naturalist's, and each must accost his side with a first love, before use has worn off the bloom and seduced their vision.

Goethe said of Aristotle that "he had better observed nature than any modern, but was too rash in his inferences and conclusions"; and he adds, "we must go to work slowly, and more indulgently with Nature, if we would get anything from her."

Inspired by his example of dealing thus reverently and lovingly with nature, the great naturalists of our time are reading secrets hitherto hidden from less careful and pious observers. If the results thus far have not satisfied the idealist, it becomes him to consider that his methods are the reverse of theirs, and that when they shall have tracked Life in its manifold shapes and modes of working in nature up to Spirit, their office is fulfilled, their work complete, and their discoveries are passed over to him for a higher generalization and genesis. "A physical delineation of nature," says Humboldt, "terminates at the point where the sphere of intellect begins, and a new world is opened to our view; it marks the limit, but does not pass it."

Whether man be the successor or predecessor of his inferiors in nature, is to be determined by exploring faithfully the realms of matter and of spirit alike, and complementing the former in the latter. Whether surveyed in order descending or ascending, in genesis or

process, from the side of the idealist or of the naturalist, the keystone of the arch in either case is an
ideal, underpropped by matter or upheld by mind.

> "If men be worlds, there is in every one
> Something to answer in fit proportion
> All the world's riches, and in substance this, —
> PERSON his form's form, and soul's soul, is."

Man, the sum total of animals, transcends all in
being a Person, a responsible creature. "The distinguishing mark," says Aristotle, "between man and
the lower animals is this : that he alone is endowed with
the power of knowing good and evil, justice and injustice, and it is a participation in this that constitutes a
family and a city." Man is man in virtue of being a
Person, a self-determining will, held accountable to
a spiritual Ideal. To affirm that brute creatures are
endowed with freedom and choice, the sense of respon-
sibility, were to exalt them into a spiritual existence
and personality ; whereas, it is plain enough that they
are not above deliberation and choice, but below it,
under the sway of Fate, as men are when running
counter to reason and conscience. The will bridges
the chasm between man and brute, and frees the fated
creature he were else. Solitary, not himself, the
victim of appetite, inmate of the den, is man till freed
from individualism, and delivered into his free Personality. "Ye must be born again."

The conflict between man's desires and satisfactions declares his defection from Personal holiness. While at one personally with himself, life suffices, his wants are seconded as they rise, and his self-respect preserved inviolate. But lapsed from personal rectitude, fallen out of and below himself, he is at variance with things around as within, his senses deceive, his will is divided, and he becomes the victim of duplicities, discontents, the prey of remorse.

"'T is a miserable thing," says Glanvil, " to have been happy; and a self-contented wretchedness is a double one. Had felicity always been a stranger to humanity, our present misery had not been. And had not ourselves been the authors of our ruin, less. We might have been made unhappy; but since we are miserable, we chose it. He that gave our outward enjoyments might have taken them from us, but none could have robbed us of innocence but ourselves. While man knows no sin, he is ignorant of nothing that it imports humanity to know; but when he has sinned, the same transgression that opens his eyes to see his own shame, shuts them against most things else but that, and the newly-purchased misery. With the nakedness of his body, he sees that of his soul, and the blindness and disarray of his faculties to which his former innocence was a stranger; and that which shows them to him makes them. No longer the creature he was made, he loses not only his Maker's image, but his own. And does not much more transcend the creatures placed at his feet, than he comes short of his ancient self."

Whose the decree
Souls Magdalens must be
To know felicity,   •
The path to it
Through pleasure's pit,
Soft sin undress
Them of their holiness, —
Hath heaven so writ?

Happier the fate
That opes heaven's gate
With crystal key
Of purity,
And thus fulfils life's destiny.

AUGUST.

" . . . The milder sun
Does through a fragrant zodiac run,
And as it works the industrious bee
Computes its time as well as we:
How can such sweet and wholesome hours
Be reckoned but with fruits and flowers?"

— Marvell.

PLATO'S LETTERS.

DAYS like these give dignity and loveliness to the landscape; the scene enhanced by imperial tints of gold and purple, the orchards bending with their ruddy burdens. It is the season of nectar and ambrosia, and suggests the Platonic bees, the literature and conversation of the Academy and Lyceum.

Very interesting reading these letters of Plato, and a goodly volume to hold in one's hand, in antique type and binding. Whether a reprint would reward the publisher, I cannot say. His seventh letter is an affecting piece of autobiography, and, taken with Plutarch's Dion, gives the best picture of his journeys to Syracuse that history affords.

"For it is a thing," he writes to the Kindred and Friends of Dion, "altogether correct and honorable for him who aspires after things the most honorable, both to himself and his country, to suffer whatever he may suffer; for not one of us is naturally immortal; nor

if this should happen to any one would he become
happy, as it seems he would to the multitude. For in
things inanimate there is nothing either good or evil
worthy of mention, but good or ill will happen to each
soul, either existing with the body, or separated from it.
But it is ever requisite to trust really to the sacred accounts of the olden times, which inform us that the soul
is immortal, and has judges of its conduct, and suffers
the greatest punishments when liberated from the body.
Hence, it is requisite to think it is a lesser evil to
suffer, than to commit the greatest sins and injuries."

.   .   .   .

"And I should have felt more justly against those
who murdered Dion, an anger, in a certain manner,
almost as great as against Dionysius; for both had
injured myself and all the rest, so to say, in the highest
degree. For the former had destroyed a man who was
willing to make use of justice; while the latter was
unwilling to make use of it through the whole of his
dominions, although possessing the highest power. In
which dominions had philosophy and power existed
really, as it were, in the same dwelling, they would
have set up amongst men, both Greeks and barbarians,
an opinion not vainly shining, and in every respect the
true one, that neither a state nor a man can ever be
happy unless by leading a life with prudence in subjection to justice, whether possessing those things themselves, or by being brought up in the habits of holy
persons, their rulers, or instructed in justice."

"This injury did Dionysius inflict. But the rest would have been a trifling wrong as compared to these. But he who murdered Dion did not know that he had done the same deed as Dionysius. For I clearly know, as far as possible for one man to speak confidently of another, that if Dion had attained power, he would never have changed it to any other form of government than to that by which he first caused Syracuse, his own country, after he had delivered it from slavery, to look joyous, and had put it into the garb of freedom; and after all this, he would by every contrivance have adorned the citizens with laws both befitting and best; and he would have been ready to do what followed in due order after this, and have colonized the whole of Sicily, and have freed it from the barbarians, by expelling some and subduing others, more easily than Hiero did. But if these things had taken place through a man just, brave, and temperate, and who was a philosopher, the same opinion of virtue would have been produced amongst the multitude, as would have been amongst all men, so to say, and have saved Dionysius, had he been persuaded by me. But now some dæmon, surely, or some evil spirit, falling upon with iniquity and impiety, and what is the greatest matter, with the audacity of ignorance, in which all evils are rooted, and from which they spring up, and afterwards produce fruit the most bitter to those who have begotten it, — this has a second time subverted and destroyed everything. However, let us, for the sake of a good augury, keep for the third time a well-omened silence." *

One sees the noble spirit of Plato in these passages, and feels how the death of his friend and pupil, Dion, at the moment when he had won the freedom of his country, and a sphere for proving his master's ideas in its rule, must have affected Plato, and the friends of Dion. If doubts have been entertained as to the genuineness of these letters, it is plain they were written by some intimate friend of his, or of Dion, and have the merit, at least, of historical accuracy and evidence.

---

* "The great interest is not in the present city of Syracuse" (writes a traveller, Feb. 9, 1869), "but in its vicinity, where we inspect the doings of Greeks twenty-five to three thousand years ago, and of the Romans at a later date. Their works are constructed out of the solid rock, and have withstood the terrible earthquakes which have completely destroyed all traces of other works. Among the interesting objects in the city is the cathedral, formerly the temple of Minerva, which is a magnificent specimen of Doric architecture, and has continued to be a place of worship through all the changes of idolatry and Christianity, for twenty-five hundred years; the church of St. Marcian here puts in its claim to have been the first church in Europe in which Christian worship was celebrated   Full of interest are the catacombs and the ancient prisons in the quarries from which the materials of Syracuse were taken; here is the Ear of Dionysius, the tyrant of Syracuse, a prison so arranged that every word spoken within it was re-echoed into his chamber, where it is said he passed entire days listening to the complaints of his victims. Here, too, is the famous fountain of Arethusa, one of the Nereads, and whom Virgil reckons among the Sicilian nymphs, as the divinity who inspired pastoral poetry. Syracuse was at different periods the residence of Plato, Simonides, Zeno, and Cicero; it was the place where Hicetus first propounded the true revolution of the earth; it was the birthplace of the poets Theocritus and Moschus, and the philosopher Archimedes, who lost his life at the capture of the city by the Romans."

PLATO.*

It was a common speech among the Athenians, that Apollo begat Æsculapius and Plato, — the one to cure bodies, the other, souls. Certainly the last was of divine extraction; his life and thoughts fruitful in genius and immortality. Like other superior persons, his birth is traced to a divine ancestry, and dignified with fables. His mother, Perictione, was a descendant of Solon, and a woman of extraordinary beauty. Aristo, his father, was of an eminent family. To him Apollo appeared in a dream, enjoining upon him respect for his wife's maternity; and, in accordance with the vision, it was affirmed, —

> " He did not issue from a mortal bed;
> A god his sire, a godlike life he led."

Whilst he was yet an infant, carried in his mother's arms, Aristo went to Hymettus to sacrifice to the Muses, taking his wife and child with him. As they were busied in the divine rites, she laid the babe in a thicket of myrtles hard by, to whom, as he slept, came a swarm of bees, artists of Hymettian honey, flying and buzzing about him, and (so runs the myth) made a honeycomb in his mouth, — this being a presage of the singular sweetness of his future eloquence foreseen in infancy.

As things fall out, not by chance, but by divine ordi-

---

* Born B. C. 429; died 348.

10

nation, and are intimated in advance, for the most part, so Socrates, who was to win the noblest of the Athenian youths for his pupil and disciple, dreamed, the night before Plato was commended to him, that a young swan fled from Cupid's altar in the Academy, and sat upon his lap, thence flew up to heaven, delighting both gods and men with its music. Next day, as he was relating this to some of his friends, Aristo came to him, and presented his son Plato to be his pupil. As soon as Socrates saw him, reading in his looks his ingenuity, " Friends," said he, " this is the swan of Cupid's Academy."

Whilst a child, he was remarkable for his sharpness of apprehension, and the admirable modesty of his disposition ; the beginnings of his youth being seasoned with labor and love of study, which virtues increased and harmonized with all others when he came to man's estate. He early learned the art of wrestling, and became so great a proficient that he took part in the Isthmian and Pythian games. As in years and virtue, so likewise he increased extraordinarily in bodily proportion and shape, insomuch that Aristo named him Plato, which implies breadth of shoulders and bold eloquence. He also studied painting and poetry, writing epics after the manner of Homer ; but, finding how far he fell short of him, he committed them to the flames. Intending to contest for the palm at the Olympic Theatre, he wrote some dramatic pieces, and gave them to the players, to be performed at the festivals. But the

day before these were to have been presented, chancing
to hear Socrates discourse in the theatre before the
Bacchanals, he was so taken with him that he not only
forbore to contest at the time, but wholly gave over all
tragic poetry, and burned his verses. From that time,
being then in his twentieth year, he became a follower
of Socrates, and studied philosophy.

He studied eight years with Socrates, committing, as
was the custom with his scholars, the substance of his
master's discourses to writing. Of these were some of
his Dialogues afterwards composed, with such additions
of argument and ornament that Socrates, hearing him
recite his Lysis, exclaimed, " O Hercules ! how many
things this young man fables of me ! "

He was one of the youngest of the Senate at the
time of Socrates' arraignment. The judges being much
displeased with Socrates, Plato took the orator's chair,
intending to plead in his master's defence, beginning,
" Though I, Athenians, am the youngest of those that
come to this place," — but, as all the Senate were
against his speaking, he was constrained to leave the
chair. Socrates being condemned, Plato offered to
obtain the money for purchasing his liberty, which
Socrates refused. Upon the death of Socrates, Plato,
— whose excessive grief is mentioned by Plutarch, —
with others of his disciples, fearing the tyranny of
those who put their master to death, fled to Euclid at
Megara, who befriended and entertained them till the
storm was blown over. He afterwards travelled in

Italy, where he addicted himself to the discipline of Pythagoras, which, though he saw it replenished with curious and high reason, yet he chiefly affected the continence and chastity, along with the knowledge of nature, possessed by that school.

Desiring to add to the knowledge of the Pythagoreans the benefits of other disciplines, he went to Cyrene to learn geometry of Theodorus, the mathematician; thence into Egypt, under pretence of selling oil, — the scope of his journey thither being to bring the knowledge of astrology from thence, and to be instructed in the rites of the prophets and the mysteries. Having taken a full survey of the country, he settled himself at Sais, learning of the school of wise men there the doctrines of the universe, the immortality of the soul, and its transmigrations. From Egypt he returned to Tarentum in Italy, where he conversed with Archytas the elder, and other Pythagoreans, adding to the learning of Socrates that of Pythagoras. He would have gone also to India to study with the Magi; but the wars then raging in Asia prevented. While in Egypt he probably became familiar with the opinions of Hermes Trismegistus. That he also received some light from Moses is probable, since his laws were translated into Greek before Alexander's time, and Josephus, the Jew, affirms, " that he chiefly followed our Lawgiver." And Numenius asks, " Of philosophers, what is Plato but Moses speaking Greek?" It is known that he brought from Sicily, where he went thrice, at the invitation of

Dionysius the younger, the three books of Philolaus, the Pythagorean, on natural philosophy, the first that were published out of that school. These he appears to have woven into his dialogue entitled "Timeus." Timeon accuses him of this appropriation.

> "You Plato with the same affection caught
> With a great sum, a little treatise bought,
> Where all the knowledge which you own was taught," —

alluding to his having received of Dionysius above eighty talents, and being flush with his money.

He is said to owe much to Protagoras, and wrote a dialogue under that title. In politics, as in morals, he drew largely from the opinions of his master, Socrates; and it is related that he was indebted to the books of Sophron, which, having been long neglected, were by him first brought to Athens, and found under his pillow at his death. Certainly he, of all scholars, had the best right to borrow, since none could recognize his own in his pages, and any author might glory in being esteemed worthy of lending a syllable to so consummate a creator.

On returning to Athens from his Egyptian travels, he settled himself in the Academy, a gymnasium, or place of exercise, in the suburbs of the city, surrounded by woods, and taking its name from Academus, one of the heroes.

> "The fluent, sweet-tongued sage first led the way,
> Who writes as smoothly as from some green spray
> Of Academe grasshoppers chirp their lay."

The occasion of his living here was that he owned an orchard adjoining the Academy. In process of time, this orchard was much enlarged by good-will, studious persons bequeathing of their riches to the professors of philosophy, to maintain the quiet and tranquillity of a philosophical life. Here he first taught philosophy; afterwards in the Gardens of Colonus. At the entrance of his school was written, —

"Let none ignorant of geometry enter here";

signifying, by this inscription, not only the proportion and harmony of lines, but also of inward affections and ideas.

His school took the name of the Academy. He thought it was a great matter, in the education of youth, to accustom them to take delight in good things; otherwise, he affirmed, pleasures were the bait of evil. Education should be conducted with a serene sweetness, never by force or violence, but by gentleness, accompanied with persuasion and every kind of invitation. His teaching was conducted by conversation or dialogue. His method of discourse was threefold, — first, to declare what that is which is taught; then, for what reason it is asserted, whether as a principal cause, or as a comparison, and whether to defend the tenet, or controvert it; thirdly, whether it be rightly said. He expounded the things which he conceived to be true; confuted those which were false; suspended his opinions on those which were doubtful.

His philosophy comprised the elements of the school of Heraclitus, Pythagoras, and Socrates, combined in a system which he distributed into three parts, — moral, consisting of action; natural, in contemplation; rational, in distinction of true and false, which, though useful in all, yet belongs to pure thought. As of old, in a tragedy the chorus acted alone; then Thespis, making some intermissions of the chorus, introduced one actor, Æschylus a second, Sophocles a third; in like manner, philosophy was at first but of one kind, — physic; then Socrates added ethic; thirdly, Plato, inventing dialectic, made it perfect.

This third part, dialectic, consisting in reason and dissertation, he treated thus: Though judgments arise from the sense, yet the judgment of truth is not in the senses. The mind alone is the judge of things, and only fit to be credited, because the mind alone sees that which is simple, uniform, and certain, which is named Idea. All sense he conceived to be obtuse and slow, and nowise able to perceive those things which seem subject to sense; those things being so minute that they cannot fall under sense; so movable and various, that nothing is one, constant and the same; all are in continual alteration and movement, and subjects of opinion only. Science he affirmed to be nowhere but in the reasons and thoughts of the mind, whose objects are ideas, whence he approved definitions of things, and applied these to whatsoever subject he discussed, discriminating things and naming them etymologically.

In this consisted the discipline of dialectic; that is, of speech concluded by reason. Though Socrates practised conversation by way of question and answer, or dialogue, yet Plato so much refined the form, both in speech and composition, that he deserves to be preferred before others, as well for invention as reformation. The analytical method, which reduces the thing sought into its principle, is his invention.*

Several words were also introduced by him in philosophy. Of these are " element," which before his time was confounded with " principle." He distinguished them thus: " Principle is that which has nothing before it whereof it might be generated; elements are compounded." The word " poem " was first used by him.

---

* " Plato," says Grote, "appreciated dialogue, not only as the road to a conclusion, but for the mental discipline and suggestive influences of the tentative and verifying process. It was his purpose to create in his hearers a disposition to prosecute philosophical researches of their own, and at the same time to strengthen their ability of doing this with effect. This remark is especially confirmed in the two dialogues, the Sophisticus and Politicus, wherein he defends himself against reproaches seemingly made at the time. To what does all this tend? Why do you stray so widely from your professed topic? Could you not have reached the point by a shorter road? He replies by distinctly proclaiming — that the process, with its improving influence on the mind, stands first in his thoughts, the direct conclusion of the inquiry only second; that the special topic which he discusses, though n itself important, is nevertheless chosen primarily with a view to its effect in communicating general method and dialectical aptitude, just as a schoolmaster, when he gives out to his pupils a word to be spelt, looks mainly, not to the exactness in spelling the particular word, but to their command of good spelling generally. To form inquisitive testing minds, fond of philosophical debate as a pursuit, and looking at opinions on the negative as on the positive side, is the first object of most of Plato's dialogues: to teach positive truth, is only a secondary object." — *Grote's Plato, Vol. II, p.* 399.

So were " superficies " and " antipodes." " Divine providence," words since appropriated by Christian theologians, was first an expression of Plato's. He, too, first considered the force and efficacy of grammar as the organ of pure thought.

His school was the pride of Athens, and drew into it its most gifted youth, as well as scholars from abroad. His most distinguished disciples were Speusippus, his nephew, whom he reformed by his example and teachings, and who became eminent as a philosopher, succeeding him in the Academy; Xenocrates, whom he much loved; Aristotle, the Stagirite, whom Plato used to call a wild colt, foreseeing that he would oppose him in his philosophy, as a colt, having sucked, kicks its dam. Xenocrates was slow, Aristotle quick, in extremity; whence Plato said of them, " See what an unequal team this of mine. What an ass and horse to yoke together ! "

Isocrates the orator, and Demosthenes, were among his auditors; Dion of Syracuse was an intimate friend of his, and by his persuasions he made two journeys to Syracuse, at one of which he was sold into slavery by the tyranny of Dionysius, and being redeemed by his friend, returned to Athens, as is related by Plutarch. Xenophon was his contemporary.

At home he lived quietly in the Academy, not taking part in public affairs, the laws and customs of the Athenians not being in harmony with his ideas of republican institutions. " Princes," he said, " had no better possessions than the familiarity of such men as could not flatter, wisdom being as necessary to a prince as the soul to the body ; and that kingdoms would be most happy if either philosophers ruled, or the rulers were inspired with philosophy, since nothing is more pernicious than power and arrogance accompanied with ignorance. Subjects should be such as princes seem to be." And he held that a philosopher might retire from the commonwealth if its affairs were unjustly administered. " A just man was a perpetual magistrate."

He affirmed that philosophy was the true helper of the soul, all else but ornamental ; that nothing is more pleasing to a sound mind than to speak and hear the truth spoken, than which nothing is better or more lasting.

The study of philosophy, if it made him select in the choice of his associates, did not sour his temper, nor render him exclusive in his intercourse and fellowship with mankind. At the Olympian games, he once fell into company with some strangers who did not know him, upon whose affections he gained greatly by his affable conversation, dining and spending the day with them, never mentioning either the Academy or Socrates, only saying his name was Plato. When they came to Athens, he entertained them courteously. " Come, Plato," said the strangers, " now show us your namesake, Socrates' disciple. Take us to the Academy : recommend us to him, that we may know him." He, smiling a little, as he used, said, " I am the man."

Whereat they were greatly amazed, having conversed so familiarly with a person of that eminence, who used no boasting or ostentation, and showed that, besides his philosophical discourse, his ordinary conversation was extremely winning.

He lived single, yet soberly and chastely. So constant was he in his composure and gravity, that a youth brought up under him, returning to his parents, and hearing his father speak vehemently and loudly, said, " I never found this in Plato." He ate but once a day, or, if the second time, very sparingly, abstaining mostly from animal food. He slept alone, and much discommended the contrary practice.

Of his prudence, patience, moderation, and magnanimity, and other virtues, there are many instances recorded. When he left his school, he was wont to say, " See, youths, that you employ your idle hours usefully. Prefer labor before idleness, unless you esteem rust above brightness."

To Philedonus, who blamed him that he was as studious to learn as teach, and asked him how long he meant to be a disciple, he replied, " As long as I am not ashamed of growing better and wiser."

Being asked what difference there was between a learned man and unlearned, — " The same as betwixt a physician and patient."

To Antisthenes, making a long oration, — " You forget that discourse is to be measured by the hearer, not the speaker."

Hearing a vicious person speak in defence of another, — " This man," said he, " carries his heart in his tongue." He blamed having musicians at feasts, " to hinder discourse."

Seeing the Agregentines so magnificent in building, and luxurious in feasting, — " These people," said he, " build as if they were immortal, and eat as if they were to die instantly."

He advised " drunken and angry men to look in the glass if they would refrain from those vices," and Xenocrates, by reason of his severe countenance, " to sacrifice to the Graces."

Being desirous to wean Timotheus, the son of Canon, the Athenian general, from sumptuous military feasts, he invited him into the Academy to a plain moderate supper, such as pleasing sleep succeeds in a good temper of body. The next day, Timotheus, observing the difference, said, " They who feasted with Plato never complained the next morning."

His servant having displeased him for some offence, he said to him, " Were I not angry, I should chastise you for it." At another time, his servant being found faulty, he had him lay off his coat; and, while he stood with his hand raised, a friend coming in asked him what he was doing: " Punishing an angry man," said he. It was a saying of his, that " no wise man punishes in respect of past faults, but for preventing future ones."

On being told that some one spoke ill of him, he answered, " No matter : I will live so that none shall believe him." When asked whether there should be any record left to posterity of his actions or sayings, — " First," said he, " we must get a name, then many things follow."

Continuing a single life to his end, and not having any heirs of his own, he bequeathed his estate to his nephew, young Adimantus, the son of Adimantus, his second brother. Besides his orchard and grounds inherited or added by purchase, he left to him " three mina of silver, a golden cup, and a finger and ear-rings of gold. The gold ear-ring was one he wore when a boy, as a badge of his nobility ; and the golden cup was one of sacrifice. He left to his servants, Ticho, Bictus, and Apolloniades, Dionysius' goods." He " owed no man anything."

He died on his eighty-first birthday, for which reason the Magi at Athens sacrificed to him, as conceiving him to have been more than man, and as having fulfilled the most perfect number, nine multiplied into itself. He died of old age ; which Seneça ascribes to his temperance and diligence.

This, among other epitaphs, was inscribed on his tombstone : —

> " Earth in her bosom Plato's body hides :
> His soul amongst the deathless gods resides.
> Aristo's son, whose fame to strangers spread,
> Made them admire the sacred life he led."

Plutarch tells that Solon began the story of the

Atlantides, which he had learned of the priests of Sais, but gave it over on account of his old age and the largeness of the work. He adds that "Plato, taking the same argument as a waste piece of fertile ground fallen to him by hereditary right, manured, refined, and inclosed it with large walls, porches, and galleries, such as never any fable had before; but he too, undertaking it late, died before completing it. 'The more things written delight us, the more they disappoint us,' he remarks, 'when not finished.' For as the Athenian city left the temple of Jupiter, so Plato's wisdom, amongst many writings, left the Atlantides alone imperfect."

The order in which his dialogues were written is yet a question of dispute with scholars. It is conceded, however, that the "Republic" and the "Laws" were completed, if not wholly written, in his old age. Nor is the number of his dialogues accurately determined. Some attributed to him are supposed to be spurious, as are some of the letters. All are contained in Bohn's edition of the works of Plato, and accessible in scholarly translations to the English reader.*

Of the great minds of antiquity, Plato stands preeminent in breadth and beauty of speculation. His

---

* Among the works deserving of a wider circulation is Thomas Stanley's "History of Philosophy." It well repays perusal, compiled as it was by an enthusiastic student of ancient thought, from reliable sources, and embodying, in an attractive style, "the Lives, Opinions, Actions, and Discourses of the Philosophers of every Sect, illustrated with Portraits of many of them. Third edition. Folio, pp. 750. London, 1701." The preceding notes are mostly extracted from this history.

books are the most suggestive, sensible, the friendliest, and, one may say, most modern of books. And it almost atones for any poverty of thought in our time, this admission to a mind thus opulent in the grandeur and graces of intelligence, giving one a sense of his debt to genius and letters. His works are a cosmos, as Pythagoras named the world. And one rises from their perusal as if returned from a circumnavigation of the globe of knowledge, human and divine. So capacious was his genius, so comprehensive, so inclusive, so subtile, and so versatile, withal, that he readily absorbed the learning of his time, moulding this into a body of beauty and harmony compact; working out, with the skill and completeness of a creator, the perfect whole we see. His erudition was commensurate with his genius, and he the sole master of his tools; since in him we have an example, as successful as it was daring, of an endeavor to animate and give individuality to his age in the persons whose ideas gave birth to the age itself. And fortunate it was for him, as for his readers, that he had before him a living illustration of his time in the person of the chief character in his dialogues, Socrates himself.

Of these dialogues, the "Republic" is the most celebrated, embodying his ripest knowledge. It fables a city planted in the divine ideas of truth and justice as these are symbolized in human forms and natural things. And one reads with emotions of surprise at finding so much of sense and wisdom embodied in a form so fair, and of such wide application, as if it were suited to all peoples and times. Where in philosophic literature is found a structure of thought so firmly fixed on natural foundations, and placing beyond cavil or question the supremacy of mind over matter, portraying so vividly the passage of ideas through the world, and thus delivering down a divine order of society to mankind? *

In reading his works, one must have the secret of his method. Written, as these are, in the simplest style of composition, his reader may sometimes weary of the slow progress of the argument, and lose himself in the devious windings of the dialogue. But this is the sole subtraction from the pleasure of perusal, — the voluminous sacrifices thus made to method: so much given to compliment, to dulness, in the interlinked threads of the golden colloquy. Yet Plato rewards as none other; his regal text is everywhere charged with lively sense, flashing in every line, every epithet, episode, with the rubies and pearls of universal wisdom. And the reading is a coronation †

---

* If his "Republic" and "Laws" hardly justify him against those who accused him of having written a form of government which he could persuade none to practise, it may be said, in his favor, that he gave laws to the Syracusians and Cretans, refusing the like to the Ayreneans and Thebans, saying, "It was difficult to prescribe laws to men in prosperity."

† "The philosophy of the fourth century, B. C.," says Grote, "is peculiarly valuable and interesting, not merely from its intrinsic speculative worth, — from the originality and grandeur of its two principal heroes, Plato and Aristotle, — from its coincidence with the full display of dramatic, rhetorical, artistic genius, but also from a fourth reason not unimportant

Plato's views of social life are instructive. His idea of woman, of her place and function, should interest women of our time. They might find much to admire, and less to criticise than they imagine. His opinions were greatly in advance of the practice of his own time, and, in some important particulars, of ours, and which, if carried into legislation, would favorably affect social purity. His proposition to inflict a fine on bachelors, and deny them political privileges, is a compliment to marriage, showing in what estimate he held that relation. So his provision for educating the children, and giving women a place in the government of the republic,

---

because it is purely Hellenic; preceding the development of Alexandrian and the amalgamation of Oriental veins of thought, with the inspirations of the Academy and the Lyceum. The Orentes and the Jordan had not yet begun to flow westward, and to impart their own color to the waters of Attica and Latium. Not merely the real, but also the ideal, world present to the minds of Plato and Aristotle, were purely Hellenic. Even during the century immediately following, this had ceased to be fully true in respect to the philosophers of Athens; and it became less and less true with each succeeding century. New foreign centres of rhetoric and literature, Asiatic and Alexandrian Hellenism, were fostered into importance by regal enactments. Plato and Aristotle are thus the special representatives of genuine Hellenic philosophy. The remarkable intellectual ascendancy acquired by them in their day and maintained over succeeding centuries, was one main reason why the Hellenic vein was enabled so long to maintain itself, though in impoverished condition, against adverse influences from the East, ever increasing in force. Plato and Aristotle outlasted all their pagan successors, — successors at once less purely Hellenic and less gifted. And when St. Jerome, near seven hundred and fifty years after the decease of Plato, commemorated with triumph the victory of unlettered Christians over the accomplishments and genius of paganism, he illustrated the magnitude of the vi tory by singling out Plato and Aristotle as the representatives of vanquished philosophy."
—*Grote's Preface to Life of Plato.*

after they had given citizens to it, are hints of our modern infant schools and woman's rights movements. His teachings on social reform generally are the best of studies, in some respects more modern than the views of our time, — anticipating the future legislation of communities. On the matter of race and temperament he thought profoundly, comprehending as have few of our naturalists the law of descent, complexions, physiognomical features and characteristics.

SOCRATES.

"Socrates," says Grote, "disclaimed all pretensions to wisdom. He announced himself as a philosopher, that is, as ignorant, yet as painfully conscious of his ignorance and anxiously searching for wisdom as a correction to it, while most men were equally ignorant, but unconscious of their ignorance, believed themselves to be already wise, and delivered confident opinions without ever having analyzed the matters on which they spoke. The conversation of Socrates was intended, not to teach wisdom, but to raise men out of this false persuasion of wisdom, which he believed to be the natural state of the human mind, into that mental condition which he called philosophy.

"His 'Elenchus' made them conscious of their ignorance, and anxious to escape from it, and prepared for mental efforts in search of knowledge ; in which search Socrates assisted them, but without declaring, and even professing inability to declare, where the truth lay in which this search was to end. He considered this change itself a great and serious improvement, converting what was evil, radical, ingrained, into evil superficial and moveable, which was a preliminary condition to any positive acquirement. The first thing to be done was to create searchers after truth, men who look at the subject for themselves, with earnest attention, and make up their own individual convictions. Even if nothing ulterior were achieved, that alone would be a great deal.

" Such was the scope of the Socratic Conversation, and such the conception of philosophy (the peculiarity which Plato borrowed from Socrates), which is briefly noted in the passage of the Lysis and developed in the Platonic dialogues, especially in the Symposeum."

Observe how confidently the great master of Dialectic went into the discussion, dealing directly all the while with the Personality of his auditors, and driving straight through the seeming windings of the discourse at the seats of thought and of sensibility, by his searching humor, his delightful irony, thus making the mind the mind's guest and querist in his suggestive colloquy. Affecting perhaps to know less than any, he yet showed those with whom he conversed how little they knew, while professing to know so much, convicting them of being ignorant of their own ignorance, real wisdom beginning in humility and openness to instruction. If he puzzled and perplexed, it was but to reduce their

egotism and ignorance, and prepare them for receiving
the truths he had to lay open in themselves.   Plato,
Aristotle, the German Methodists, but define and deliver the steps of his method.

BERKELEY.

Of modern philosophic writers, Berkeley has given
the best example of the Platonic Dialogue, in his
" Minute Philosopher," a book to be read with profit, for
its clearness of thought and method.   His claim to the
name of metaphysician transcends those of most of his
countrymen.   He, first of his nation, dealt face to face
with ideas as distinguished from scholastic fancies and
common notions, and thus gave them their place in the
order of mind ; and this to exhaustive issues, as his
English predecessors in thought had failed to do.   His
idealism is the purest which the British Isles have produced.   Platonic as were Cudworth, Norris, Henry More,
in cast of thought less scholastic than Taylor of Nor-
wich, — who was an exotic, rather, transplanted from
Alexandrian gardens, — Berkeley's thinking is indigenous, strong in native sense and active manliness.   His
works are magazines of rare and admirable learning,
subtleties of speculation, noble philanthropies.   They
deserve a place in every scholar's library, were it but to
mark the fortunes of thought, and accredit the poet's
admiring line : —

"To Berkeley every virtue under heaven."

BOEHME.

WRITE to Walton, the British Boehmist, whose letters interest by the information they contain of himself and of his literary ventures. Any disciple of the distinguished Mystic and student of his works, living in foggy London in these times, is as significant and noteworthy as are students of Hegel in St. Louis.* Mysticism is the sacred spark that has lighted the piety and illuminated the philosophy of all places and times. It has kindled especially and kept alive the profoundest thinking of Germany and of the continent since Boehme's first work, "The Aurora," appeared. Some of the deepest thinkers since then have openly acknowledged their debt to Boehme, or secretly borrowed without acknowledgment their best illustrations from his writings. It is conceded that his was one of the most original and subtlest of minds, and that he has exercised a deeper influence on the progress of thought than any one since Plotinus. Before Bacon, before Newton, Swedenborg, Goethe, he gave theories of. nature, of the signatures of colors and

---

* A mystic book entitled "Quinquenergia, or Proposals for a new Practical Theology," by Henry S. Sutton, was published in London in 1854. Mr. Sutton is plainly tinctured with Boehme's theosophy, if not a disciple of his as appears from his book. It is a volume of singular originality, and the latest modern attempt at a Genesis from First Principles that I have met with. It seems to have attracted few readers in England or in this country.

forms, of the temperaments, the genesis of sex, the lapse
of souls, and of the elementary worlds. He stripped life
of its husk, and delivered its innermost essence. Instead
of mythology, he gave, if not science, the germs, if
nothing more. And when the depths of his thinking
have been fathomed by modern observers it will be soon
enough to speak of new revelations and arcanas. His
teeming genius is the genuine mother of numberless
theories since delivered, from whose trunk the natural
sciences have branched forth and cropped out in scientific
systems. And like Swedenborg, it has borne a theology,
cosmology, illustrious theosophists and naturalists, —
Law, Leibnitz, Oken, Schelling, Goethe, Baader, and
other philosophers of Germany.

His learned English disciple and translator, Rev.
William Law, an author once highly esteemed and much
read by a former generation of pietists, says of him in
his Introduction to Boehme's Works : —

"Whatsoever the great Hermes delivered in ora-
cles, or Pythagoras spoke by authority, or Socrates
or Aristotle affirmed, whatever divine Plato prophesied,
or Plotinus proved, — this and all this, or a far higher
and profounder philosophy, is contained in Boehme's
writings. "And if there be any friendly medium that
can possibly reconcile these ancient differences between
the divine Wisdom that has fixed her place in Holy
Writ and her stubborn handmaid, natural Reason, — this
happy marriage of the Spirit of God and the soul, this
wonderful consent of discords in harmony, — we shall

find it in great measure in Boehme's books ; only let not
the non or misunderstanding of the most rational reader
(if not a little sublimed above the sphere of common
reason) be imputed as a fault to this elevated philosopher, no more than it was to the divine Plotinus, whose
scholars, even after much study, failed to comprehend
many of his doctrines."

Dr. Henry More, with a qualifying discrimination of
Law's estimate, writes : —

" Jacob Boehme, I conceive, is to be reckoned in the
number of those whose imaginative faculty has the pre-
eminence above the rational, and though he was a holy
and good man, his natural complexion, notwithstanding,
was not destroyed but retained its property still, and
therefore his imagination being very busy about divine
things, he could not without a miracle fail of becoming
an enthusiast, and of receiving divine truths upon the
account of the strength and vigor of his fancy, which
being so well qualified with holiness and sanctity, proved
not unsuccessful in sundry apprehensions, but in others
it fared with him after the manner of men, the sagacity
of his imagination failing him, as well as the anxiety
of reason, does others of like integrity with himself."*

---

* Students of Boehme have been few and far between. Edward Taylor
appears to have been Boehme's most distinguished disciple in England
before William Law. He published " A Compendious View of the Teutonic
Philosophy." London, 1670. Also Jacob Boehme's " Philosophy Unfolded
in divers Considerations and Demonstrations, and a Short Account of his
Life." London, 1690. John Sparrow published Boehme's Tracts and
Epistles. London, 1662. John Pordage's " Theologia Mystica, or the Mystic Divinity of the Eternal Invisibles," London, 1683, is a rare volume.

MR. WALTON'S LETTER.

" By Theosophy I understand the true science of Deity, Nature, and Creature. There are two classes of theosophists, or true mystic philosophers. The one such as Gichtel, the editor of the first German edition of Jacob Boehme (whose letters and life in seven volumes are now being translated into English, and if the necessary funds can be raised they will be printed.) Gichtel truly experimented the regenerated life of Christianity according to the science thereof contained in Boehme's writings ; Bramwell fathomed Christianity according to the simple *prima facie* representation thereof in the Gospel ; in like manner in another form Terstegan was also a high proficient therein, as were also some of the ancient mystics and ascetics of France, Spain, and Germany, as referred to in the Cyclopedia. In the path of Gichtel there have been few and remote followers.

" The other class is composed of those who have intellectually fathomed the scope of Boehme's philosophy, such as Freher, Law, Lee, Pordage, and others.

" As to the pretended independent ' seers,' outsiders of Boehme's revelations, — whose names need not be mentioned, — these are of course not to be admitted into the category of the standard theologists, being mere phantasmatists or visionaries, and who, though uttering a great many good, and to some recondite minds, surprising things, say in effect nothing but what is to be found in a much more solid and edifying form in the writings of ancient classic divines and philosophers.

" As you will see by the accompanying printed papers, I assert that for theosophy to have its true efficiency in the world, there must not only be an intellectual acquaintance with all nature, magical, mental, and physical, — all which is present in every point of sense and mental essence as revealed in Boehme, — but there must be the actual realization of the translocated principles of man's threefold being into their original corelative positions, and this in high confirmed reality; which is only another expression for the theological and alchymical term, ' regeneration.' And further, I say, there must therewith be a profound knowledge of the science and manifestation of animal magnetism.

" As to spiritism, of course at present theosophy has nothing to do with it, except to contemplate the workings of the magia of the fantasy of the grounds of nature, as shown in it.

" I may just observe, that, if you are not acquainted with the facts, you will find in V. Schubert, a German Professor, some most interesting interpretations of and deductions from Boehme's philosophy. He is a truly ingenious elucidator of many of nature's secrets purely from his conception of Boehme, and for general reading in theosophy, is much more interesting than Baader, who is very technical. But, as for myself, I cannot derive from these or any other authors, what my under-

11

standing requires that is beyond the manuscripts and printed authors in my sole possession. Those I have, contain the philosophy of nature and creation far more lucidly and classically opened than is found in any modern publication, for it is fundamentally demonstrated therein ; whereas in Hamburger and others, Boehme is merely systematized, leaving his profundities in their original abyss, like ore in the mine ; whereas my authors work it all out as far as they could in their day.

" I am and have been long engaged in preparing a compendium of the true principles of all Being, and setting forth all its stages up to the present time : all which is a great mystery both to philosophy and science, as you are doubtless aware. It has never yet been done, and is indeed the grand desideratum. We have never yet been able to reconcile the seeming or allowed declaration of Scripture concerning the creation, with the Newtonian philosophy, and the disclosures of modern chymic, electric, and other sciences, so as to present a solid, united, and convincing chain of the history of nature from the first point of mental essence, to the present state of physical things. And yet there must be such a history and knowledge thereof, latent in the human mind, and in the present daylight of theosophy and physical science, capable of being educed thereout, in a manner commending itself on the sight of it, with almost the force of self-evidence, though in some points appearing to clash with the seeming sense of Scripture.

" My labors are in the preparation of a series of symbolic illustrations (like Quarle's Emblems), whereby, with the accompanying text, to produce this kind of self-evident conviction. Of course I only open the procedure to the present time. You may conceive the time and labor and expense entailed by such an effort. Also the fierce daily long discussions with an avowed and actual rationalist opponent, whom I have for the purpose, without which the truth or science cannot be made to rise up apprehensively in the mind, and then only in a mind in which theosophical and modern scientific knowledge is, as it were, all in living activity, like a magic looking-glass, wherein the images are all living, and can be called forth instantly into visibility, as required by the formula of each successive consideration arising in the discussion, or during private meditation and reading of Boehme, having an object in view.

" The science of all things lies in the Mind. In Newton this plant of Jacob Boehme was largely cultivated for his day ; but now, by means of modern science, the true history of all being can be brought forth as a complete logical tree. And this is what the world wants, a perfect philosophy and a perfect theology, as one only sound of the word of nature. This was the divine object in giving the last dispensation through Boehme, though this was such a chaos yet unavoidable. From which revelation of the ground and mystery of all things have ensued all the grand regenerating discoveries of modern science, as I have shown, and can now more fully demonstrate. All date from that new opened puncture of divine light in Boehme.

" I may just mention that I have a collection of all the chief editions of Boehme, in German, Dutch, English, and French, together with other elucidations whereby to produce a new and most harmonious edition of Boehme. Indeed such a thing cannot be accomplished without the means in my possession. I also have at command with me the literary and critical knowledge requisite to produce a correct translation. For there are numerous errors of sense in the German as in the English copies. Indeed in some cases the sense of the passage is not apprehensible. I trust the world will call for this work before I die, in order that I may have the pleasure of preparing, or rather directing, its accomplishment. If I can procure a copy of the Cyclopedia you write about, I shall be happy to present it to you.*

" I am, dear Sir, Yours very truly,

" CHRISTOPHER WALTON.

"LONDON, 15th February, 1868."

" The object of these publications," says Mr. Walton, in his Prospectus, " and of their distribution in the libraries of Great Britain and the United States, is to induce and promote in a general manner, the study of

---

* The " Cyclopedia of Pure Christian Theology and Theosophic Science," is to contain the works of Boehme and his distinguished followers, Freher, Gechtel, Pordage, Lee, Law, and others. The first volume is already printed for private circulation, and deposited in the chief libraries of Europe and America. It contains six hundred and eighty-eight closely printed pages, chiefly of exposition and comment on Boehme, with biographical accounts of Boehmists and of their works interspersed in voluminous notes.

pure metaphysical science, commencing at its root and ground in Deity, thence through all those principles of nature, eternal and temporal, of mind, spirit, and body, which develop and concentre themselves in the form, constitution, and support of man, as such, with a view to render it subservient to its true end and design, namely, the radical purification of theology throughout the earth, and the final resolution of it into a fixed and progressive science, and art in its kind, as contemplated and provided for by Christianity."

For those interested in the history of Mysticism, "Vaughan's Hours with the Mystics," published in London, 1856, is an interesting volume, full of information communicated by way of conversation, and in an attractive style.

CRABBE ROBINSON'S DIARY.

THURSDAY, 19.

CRABBE ROBINSON'S Diary is interesting; all he tells us of Landor, Wordsworth, Coleridge, is especially so. The book gives, perhaps, the best personal and literary picture of the times in which he lived. Few men had a wider circle of literary acquaintances than the author. His book is a real addition to contemporary literature, and shows the value of the Diary for preserving in an attractive form what would otherwise have been lost to the world. Robinson is no Boswell; he knew what to omit, what to commit to writing, gave fair transcripts of what he saw, without prepossession or prejudice.

COLERIDGE.

What Robinson tells of Coleridge is especially noticeable.

" I used," he says, " to compare him as a disputant to a serpent, — easy to kill if you assume the offensive ; but if you attack him, his bite is mortal. Some time after writing this, when I saw Madame De Stael, in London, I asked her what she thought of him. She replied, ' He is very great in monologue, but he has no idea of dialogue.' "

Perhaps not. Yet with his equal, he would not have been found wanting in this respect. Less English than German in genius, he would have been on terms of equality with thinkers of all times. But for his introduction of German ideas into English literature, we had waited a generation or more. He comprehended and interpreted the ideas and methods of its great thinkers. Better than most, he fulfilled Plato's canon, that " only the gods discriminate and define." I find him the most stimulating of modern British thinkers. He had wider sympathies with pure thought, and cast more piercing glances into its essence and laws than any contemporary.

I must repeat my sense of obligation to him for the quickening influence which the perusal of his pages always awakens, at every paragraph making me his debtor for a thought, an image, which it were worth while to have lived for, so stimulating is his phrase to imagination and reason alike; scarcely less to understanding and memory. If his mysticism tinge his speculations with its shifting hues, and one threads the labyrinth into which he conducts with wonder and amazement, he yet surrenders unreservedly to his guide, sure of coming to the light, with memorable experiences to reward him for the adventure.

His appreciation of the Greek, as of the Teutonic genius, is the more remarkable when we consider how rarely his countrymen have comprehended foreign ideas; and that Shakespeare even found in him his first interpreter.

In his Literary Remains, we find these remarkable notes on the Greek drama: —

" It is truly singular that Plato — whose philosophy and religion were both exotic at home, and a mere opposition to the finite in all things, genuine prophet and anticipator of the protestant era — should have given in his dialogue of the Banquet a justification of our Shakespeare. For he relates that, when all the other guests had either dispersed or fallen asleep, Socrates only, together with Aristophanes and Agathon, remained awake; and that, while he continued to drink with them out of a large goblet, he compelled them,

though most reluctantly, to admit that it was the business of one and the same genius to excel in tragic and
comic poetry ; or, that the tragic poet ought, at the same
time, to contain within himself the powers of comedy.
Now, as this was certainly repugnant to the entire
theory of the ancient critics, and contrary to all their
experience, it is evident that Plato must have fixed the
eye of his contemplation on the innermost essentials of
the drama, abstracted from conditions of age and country. In another passage he even adds the reason, namely :
that opposites illustrate each other's nature, and in their
struggle draw forth the strength of the combatants,
and display the conquered as sovereign even in the
territories of the rival power."

Again : " The tragic poet idealizes his characters by
giving to the spiritual part of our nature a more decided
preponderance over animal cravings and impulses than
is met with in real life ; the comic poet idealizes his
characters by making the animal the governing power,
and the intellectual the mere instrument. But as tragedy is not a collection of virtues and perfections, but
takes care only that the vices and imperfections shall
spring from the passions, errors, and prejudices which
arise of the soul ; so neither is comedy a mere
crowd of vices and follies, but whatever qualities it
represents, even though they are in a certain sense
amiable, it still displays them as having their origin in
some dependence on our lower nature, accompanied
with a defect in true freedom of spirit and self-subsist-

ence, and subject to that unconnection by contradiction of inward being, to which all folly is owing."

Coleridge, while writing this masterly analysis of the seats of the tragic and comic in man's inner being, and with the text of Plato and of Shakespeare before him, must have been contemplating the springs of his own defects, the strength twinned with his weaknesses, which ever made him the helpless demigod he was; aspiring ever, yet drawn downward by the leash of his frailties, as tragic a character as any that Shakespeare himself has drawn.

SELDEN'S TABLE TALK.

TUESDAY, 24.

" LEARNED Selden," learned in civil and political wisdom as were few of his great contemporaries. If his book of Table Talk has less repute than Bacon's famous Essays, like that, opened anywhere, it displays the author's eminent discretion, his comprehensive understanding, apposite illustration of his theme. His homely, familiar manner, has its attractions as well for the scholar as for the common reader; pregnant as are his sentences with his great good sense, rare learning, bringing abstruse subjects home to the affairs of life in a style at once perspicuous and agreeable. "He was a person," says Lord Clarendon, "whom no character can flatter, or transmit in any expressions equal to his merit. He was of such stupendous learning in all kinds of languages that a man would have thought he had been entirely conversant among books, and had never spent an hour but in reading and writing. Yet his humanity, courtesy, and affability were such, that he would have been thought to have been bred in the best courts, but that his good-nature, charity, and delight in doing good, and in communicating all he knew, exceeded his breeding. His style in all his writings seems harsh, and sometimes obscure, which is not wholly to be imputed to the abstruse subjects of which he commonly treated, but to a little undervaluing of style, and too much propensity to the language of antiquity; but in his conversation he was the most clear discourser, and had the best faculty of making hard things easy, and of presenting them to the understanding, of any man that hath been known."

Coleridge, who never let any person of eminence, in thought or erudition, escape his attention, says : " There is more weighty bullion sense in this book (The Table Talk) than I ever found in the same number of pages of any uninspired writer."

Ben Jonson addressed him thus : —

> . . . "You that have been
> Ever at home, yet have all countries seen,
> And like a compass keeping one foot still
> Upon your centre, do your circle fill
> Of general knowledge. . . .
> I wondered at the richness, but am lost
> To see the workmanship so excel the cost!

To mark the excellent seasoning of your style,
And manly elocution! not one while
With horror rough, then rioting with wit,
But to the subject still the colors fit,
In sharpness of all search, wisdom choice,
Newness of sense, antiquity of voice!
I yield, I yield. The matter of your praise
Floods in upon me, and I cannot raise
A bank against it; nothing but the round
Large clasp of nature such a wit can bound."

One's pen cannot be better drawn across paper, than in transcribing some of his wise and pithy sayings : —

" *Books.* 'T is good to have translators, because they serve as a comment, so far as the judgment of the man goes."

" Quoting of authors is most for matter of fact ; and then I cite them as I would produce a witness, sometimes for a free expression ; and then I give the author his due, and gain myself praise for reading him."

" Henry the Eighth made a law that all men might read the Scripture, except servants ; but no woman except ladies and gentlewomen who had leisure and might ask somebody the meaning. The law was repealed in Edward Sixth's days."

" Laymen have best interpreted the hard places in the Bible, such as Scaliger, Grotius, Salmasius, etc. The text serves only to guess by ; we must satisfy ourselves fully out of the authors that lived about those times."

" *Ceremony.* Ceremony keeps up all things. 'T is like a penny glass to a rich spirit, or some excellent water ; without it the water were spilt, the spirit lost."

" *Damnation.* To preach long, loud, and damnation, is the way to be cried up. We love a man that damns us, and we run after him to save us."

" *Friends.* Old friends are best. King James used to call for his old shoes, they were easiest to his feet."

" *Language.* Words must be fitted to a man's mouth. 'T was well said of the fellow that was to make a speech for my Lord Mayor : he desired to take measure of his lordship's mouth."

" *Learning.* No man is wiser for his learning ; it may administer matter to work in, or objects to work upon ; but wit and wisdom are born with a man."

" *Power.* Syllables govern the world."

" *Reason.* The reason of a thing is not to be inquired after till you are sure the thing itself is so. We commonly are at ' What 's the reason of it ? ' before we are sure of the thing. 'T was an excellent question of my Lady Cotton, when Sir Robert Cotton was magnifying of a shoe which was Moses' or Noah's, and wondering at the strange shape and fashion of it, — ' But, Mr. Cotton,' says she, ' are you sure it is a shoe ? ' "

" *Religion.* Religion is like the fashion; one man wears his doublet slashed, another laced, another plain; but every man has a doublet. So every man has his religion. We differ about trimming."

" We look after religion as the butcher did after his knife, when he had it in his mouth."

WOMAN.

SUNDAY, 29.

Ever the feminine fades into mystery,
Pales undistinguished into the powers of nature,
There working with earnest force in silence,
Bashful and beautiful in its reserves.

DIVINATION seems heightened and raised to its highest power in woman, like mercury, the more sensitive to the breath of its atmosphere; — the most delicate metre of character, as if in the finest persons, the sex predominated to give the salient graces and gifts peculiar to woman. The difference appears to be of bias, not of positive power, of thought and feeling differently disposed, and where the extremes merge towards unity, not easily discriminated. Still, each preserves its distinctive traits under all differences, neither being mistaken for the other. A woman's thought is not taken for a man's, nor the contrary; though the outward expression were the same, each preserves its sexual tone and color. Any seeming exceptions are counterfeits, and confirm the law that sentiment is feminine, thought masculine, by whomsoever expressed ; neither can blend fully and confound the other under any metamorphosis, sex being a constant factor individualizing the personality of souls. The ancient philosophers had so good an opinion of the sex, that they ascribed all sciences to the Muses, all sweetness and morality to the Graces, and prophetic inspiration to the Sibyls.

Women have been subject alike to the admiration and contempt of men. It were handsomer to quote the poet's praises than blame, the Greek poets Æschylus, Sophocles, and Euripides especially. I like to enrich my pages with some of their fine lines, and not less for the new interest taken in the sex.

Æschylus.

" Wedlock is a state preordained of Destiny, and its Obligations are more binding than an oath."

" Bite thy lips or ever thou speak words of impurity."

" Can heaven's fair beams show a fond wife a sight
More welcome than her husband from his wars
Returned with glory, when she opes the gate
And springs to welcome him."

Euripides.

" Men need not try where women fail."

" To a father waxing old
Nothing is dearer than a daughter ; sons
Have spirits of a higher pitch, but less inclined
To sweet endearing tenderness."

" Happy is it so to place
A daughter; yet it pains a father's heart
When he delivers to another's house
A child, the object of his tender care."

"A wise man in his house should find a wife
Gentle and courteous, or no wife at all."

" With silence of the tongue
And cheerfulness of look I entertained
My husband; where my province to command
I knew, and where to yield obedience to him."

" When the wife endures
The ungentle converse of a husband rude
In manners, in his person rude, to die
Were rather to be wished."

"If well accorded, the connubial state
From all its strings speaks perfect harmony;
If ill at home, abroad the harsh notes jar,
And with rude discord wound the ear of peace."

" For women are by nature formed
To feel some consolation when their tongue
Gives utterance to the afflictions they endure."

" O trebly blest the placid lot of those,
Whose hearth-foundations are in pure love laid,
Where husband's breast with tempered ardor glows,
And wife, oft mother, is in heart a maid."

Sophocles.

" Note well a house that is prosperous among men, and you
will find virtue among its women folk."

" Seek not thy fellow-citizens to guide
Till thou canst order well thine own fireside."

SEPTEMBER.

"While slowly o'er the hills
The unnerved day piles his prodigious sunshine.
Here be gardens of Hesperian mould,
Recesses rare, temples of Lirch and fern,
Perfumes of light-green sumac, ivy thick,
And old stone fences tottering to their fall,
And gleaming lakes that cool invite the bath,
And most aerial mountains for the West."

— *Channing.*

WALDEN POND.

TO Walden with May, who takes a pencil sketch for her collection. Thoreau's hermitage has disappeared, and the grounds are overgrown with pines and sumac, leaving the site hardly traceable. The shores of Walden are as sylvan as ever near Thoreau's haunt, but have been shorn of wood on the southern side. No spot of water in these parts has a more interesting history. It well deserved the poet's praises while Thoreau dwelt on its shores.

> "It is not far beyond the village church,
>   After we pass the wood that skirts the road,
>   A lake, — the blue-eyed Walden, — that doth smile
>   Most tenderly upon its neighbor pines,
>   And they as if to recompense this love,
>   In double beauty spread their branches forth.
>   This lake has tranquil loveliness and breadth,
>   And of late years has added to its charms,
>   For one attracted to its pleasant edge
>   Has built himself a little hermitage,
>   Where with much piety he passes life.

" More fitting place I cannot fancy now,
  For such a man to let the line run off
  The mortal reel, such patience hath the lake,
  Such gratitude and cheer are in the pines.
  But more than either lake or forest's depths
  This man has in himself: a tranquil man,
  With sunny sides where well the fruit is ripe,
  Good front, and resolute bearing to this life,
  And some serener virtues, which control
  This rich exterior prudence, virtues high,
  That in the principles of things are set,
  Great by their nature and consigned to him,
  Who, like a faithful merchant, does account
  To God for what he spends, and in what way.

" Thrice happy art thou, Walden ! in thyself,
  Such purity is in thy limpid springs;
  In those green shores which do reflect in thee,
  And in this man who dwells upon thy edge,
  A holy man within a hermitage.
  May all good showers fall gently into thee ;
  May thy surrounding forests long be spared,
  And may the dweller on thy tranquil shores
  Here lead a life of deep tranquillity,
  Pure as thy waters, handsome as thy shores,
  And with those virtues which are like the stars."

" When I first paddled a boat on Walden," wrote
Thoreau, " it was completely surrounded by thick and
lofty pine and oak woods, and in some spots, coves of
grape vines had run over the trees and formed bowers
under which a boat could pass. The hills which form
its shore are so steep, and the woods on them so high,

that as you looked down the pond from the west end, it had the appearance of an amphitheatre. For some kind of sylvan spectacle, I have spent many an hour when I was younger, floating over its surface as the zephyr willed, having paddled my boat to the middle, and lying on my back across the seats in a summer forenoon, and looking into the sky, dreaming awake until I was aroused by my boat touching the sand, and I arose to see what shore my fates had impelled me to. In these days, when idleness was the most attractive and productive industry, many a forenoon have I stolen away, preferring to spend thus the most valued part of the day. For I was rich, if not in money, in sunny hours and summer days, and spent them lavishly. Nor do I regret that I did not waste more of them behind a counter, or in a workshop, or at the teacher's desk, in which last two places I have spent many of them.

"I must say that I do not know what made me leave the pond. I left it as unaccountably as I went to it. To speak sincerely, I went there because I had got ready to go. I left it for the same reason.

"These woods! why do I not feel their being cut more freely? Does it not affect me nearly? The axe can deprive me of much. Concord is sheared of its pride. I am certain by the loss attached to my native town in consequence, one and a main link is broken. I shall go to Walden less frequently.

"Look out what window I will, my eyes rest in the

distance on a forest. Is this circumstance of no value? Why such pains in old countries to plant gardens and parks? A certain sample of wild nature, a certain primitiveness? The towns thus bordered with a fringe and tasselled border, each has its preservers. Methinks the town should have more supervisors to control its parks than it has. It concerns us all whether these proprietors choose to cut down all the woods this winter or not. I love to look at Ebby Hubbard's oaks and pines on the hillside from Brister's Hill, and am thankful that there is one old miser who will not sell or cut his woods, though it is said that they are wasting. 'It is an ill wind that blows nobody any good.'"

"Walk round Walden Pond these warm winter days. The wood-chopper finds that the wood cuts easier than when it had the frost in it, though it does not split so readily. Thus every change in the weather has its influence on him, and is appreciated by him in a peculiar way. The wood-cutter and his practices and experiences are more to be attended to; his accidents, perhaps, more than any others, should mark the epochs in a winter's day. Now that the Indian is gone, he stands nearest to nature. Who has written the history of his day? How far still is the writer of books from the man, his old playmate, it may be, who chops in the woods? There are ages between them. Homer refers to the progress of the wood-cutter's work to mark the time of day on the plains of Troy. And the inference from such premises commonly is, that he lived in a more primitive state of society than the present. But I think this is a mistake. Like proves like in all ages, and the fact that I myself should take pleasure in preferring the simple and peaceful labors which are always proceeding; that the contrast itself always attracts the civilized poet to what is rudest and most primitive in his contemporaries; — all this rather proves a certain interval between the poet and the wood-chopper, whose labor he refers to, than an unusual nearness to him, on the principle that familiarity breeds contempt. Homer is to be subjected to a very different kind of criticism from any he has received. That reader who most fully appreciates the poet, and derives the greater pleasure from his work, lives in circumstances most like those of the poet himself.

" This afternoon I throw off my outside coat, a mild spring day. I must hie me to the meadows. The air is full of bluebirds. The ground is almost entirely bare. The villagers are out in the sun, and every man is happy whose work takes him out-of-doors. I go by Sleepy Hollow towards the great fields. I lean over a rail to hear what is in the air, liquid with the bluebird's warble. My life partakes of infinity. The air is deep as our natures. Is the drawing in of this vital air attended with no more glorious results than I witness? The air is a velvet cushion against which I press my ear. I go forth to make new demands on life. I wish to begin this summer well. To do something in it worthy and wise. To transcend my daily routine and that of my townsmen, to have my immortality now, — that it be in the quality of my daily life, — to pay the greatest price, the greatest tax of any man in Concord, and enjoy the most! I will give all I am for my nobility. I will pay all my days for my success. I pray that the life of this spring and summer may be fair in my memory. May I dare as I have never done. May I purify myself anew as with fire and water, soul and body. May my melody not be wanting to the season. May I gird myself to be a hunter of the beautiful, that nought escape me. May I attain to a youth never attained. I am eager to report the glory of the universe: may I be worthy to do it; to have got through regarding human values, so as not to be distracted from regarding divine values. It is reasonable that a man should be something worthier at the end of the year than he was at the beginning."

A delightful volume might be compiled from Thoreau's Journals by selecting what he wrote at a certain date annually, thus giving a calendar of his thoughts on that day from year to year. Such a book would be instructive in many ways, — to the naturalist, the farmer, woodman, scholar; and as he was wont to weave a sensible moral into his writings, it would prove a suggestive treatise on morals and religion also. Not every preacher takes his text from his time, his own eyes, ears, and feet, in his sensible, superior manner.

THE IDEAL CHURCH.

MONDAY, 13.

THE divinity students come according to appointment and pass the day. It is gratifying to be sought by thoughtful young persons, especially by young divines, and a hopeful sign when graduates of our schools set themselves to examining the foundations of their faith ; the ceilings alike with underpinnings of the world's religious ideas and institutions, their genesis and history. Plainly, the drift of thinking here in New England, if not elsewhere, is towards a Personal Theism, inclusive of the faiths of all races, embodying the substance of their Sacred Books, with added forms and instrumentalities suited to the needs of our time. The least curious observer (I tell my visitors) cannot fail to see that at no previous period in our religious history, had so profound and anxious inquiries been made into the springs and foundations of spiritual truths. The signs of our time indicate that we are on the eve of a recasting of the old forms. Always there had been two divisions in the theological as in the political and social spheres, — the conservative and the radically progressive. This division marks itself at the present, so sweeping is the wave of religious speculation, not only among professed Christians, but among the thoughtful outside of churches. Wherever we look, earnest men

12

are pondering in what manner they can best serve God and man.

Let us discriminate religious truth from mere opinions. The fruit of temperament, culture, individuality, these are wont to be local, narrow, exclusive. The planting of a church to which all men can subscribe, demands a common bond of sympathy, the feeling of brotherhood, mutual respect, peculiarities, culture, respect for old and young. Such is the bond of union for the New Church. The essence of all creeds is God, Personal, Incarnate, without whom a church and divine worship were impossible. Not to enter into the metaphysics of creeds and philosophy of systems, let us sketch an outline of our Ideal Church.

Our forms are of the past, not American. Times modify forms. The world of thought moves fast; what is good for one time may ill suit another. The culture of past ages is stealing into our present thought, deepening, widening it. Sects are provincial, geographical; the coming church is to speak to every need, every power of humanity. A revelation is not a full revelation which fails to touch the whole man, quicken all his powers into beauty and strength of exercise.

First, of the architecture. Let this represent the essential needs of the soul. Our dwelling-houses best typify the tender domesticities of life; let the church edifice embody more of this familiar love. In the ordering of the congregation, let age have precedence; give the front seats to the eldest members; let families sit together, so that the element of family affection be incorporated in the worship. An arrangement of the pews in semicircles will bring all more nearly at equal gradation of distance from the speaker, whose position is best slightly elevated above the congregation. Pictures and statues, representing to the senses the grand events of the religious history of the past, may be an essential part of the church furniture; the statues embodying the great leaders of religious thought of all races. These are not many; the world owes its progress to a few persons. The divine order gives one typical soul to a race. Let us respect all races and creeds, as well as our own; read and expound their sacred books like our Scriptures. Constituting a body of comparative divinity, each is a contribution to the revelation made to mankind from time to time. Could any one well remain exclusive or local in his thought from such studies and teachings? Christianity, as the religion of the most advanced nations, is fast absorbing the beauty, the thought, the truth of other religions, and this fact should find expression also.

Let there be frequent interchange of preachers and teachers, since few can speak freshly to the same congregation for every Sunday in the year; only the freshest thought, the purest sentiments, were their due. Let the services be left to the speaker's selection. Let the music be set to the best lyrical poetry of all ages, poems sometimes read or recited as part of the services. As for prayer, it may be spoken from an over-

flowing heart, may be silent, or omitted at the option
of the minister.

Let the children have a larger share in the religious
services than hitherto ; one half of the day be appropriated to them. Who can speak to children can
address angels ; true worship is childlike. " All nations," said Luther, " the Jews especially, school their
children more faithfully than Christians. And this is
one reason why religion is so fallen. For all its hopes
of strength and potency are ever committed to the generation that is coming on to the stage. And if this is
neglected in its youth, it fares with Christianity as with
a garden that is neglected in the spring-time. There
is no greater obstacle in the way of piety than neglect
in the training of the young. If we would reinstate
religion in its former glory, we must improve and
elevate the children, as it was done in days of old." *

---

* It appears from " Letchford's Plain Dealings concerning New England,"
that the church in Concord was the first in the colony that adopted the
practice of catechising the children on Sundays. " The unmarried people,"
he says, " were also required to answer questions, after which Mr. Bulkeley
gave expositions and made applications to the whole congregation." And
this practice soon found its way into all the churches, became a part of the
Sunday service in the church, in the family at last. From these it passed,
subsequently, into the schools, a part of Saturday forenoon being devoted
to recitations, and where the parents were of different persuasions, the
teachers heard these from the Westminster, or Church of England cate-
chisms, accordingly. Some of us remember committing both to memory,
and having the benefit of so much comparative divinity as these furnished
at that early age.

COLLYER.

Our young divines may study Beecher and Collyer, if they will learn the types of preaching which the people most enjoy and flock to hear. Collyer, without pretension to eloquence, is most eloquent in his plain, homely, human way. He meets his audience as the iron he once smote, and his words have the ring of true steel. He speaks from crown to toe, and with a delightful humor that gives his rhetoric almost a classic charm, his Yorkshire accent adding to the humane quality of his thought. There is as little of scholarly pretence as of priestly assumption in his address, and he makes his way by his placid strength, clear intelligence, breadth of sympathy, putting the rhetoric of the schools to the blush.

BEECHER.

I once entered Beecher's church with a friend who was not often seen in such sanctuaries. Aisles, body, galleries, every slip, every chair, all were occupied, many left standing. The praise, the prayer, the christening, — there were a dozen babes presented for baptism, — all were devout, touching, even to tears at times. I know I wept, while my friend was restive, fancying himself, as he declared, in some Pagan fane. The services all seemed becoming, however. Here was no realm of Drowsy Head. The preaching was the more effective for its playfulness, point, strength, pertinency. Coming from the heart, the doctrine found the hearts of its hearers. The preacher showed his good sense, too, in omitting the trite phrases and traditions, speaking straight to his points in plain, homely speech, that carried the moral home to its mark. It was refreshing to get a touch of human nature, the preaching so often failing in this respect. The speaker took his audience along with him by his impetuosity, force of momentum, his wit playing about his argument, gathering power of persuasion, force of statement as he passed. His strong sense, broad humanity, abounding animal spirits, humor, anecdote, perhaps explain the secret of his power and popularity.

IDEALS.

SUNDAY, 19.

OUR instincts are idealists. Contradicting impressions of the senses, they prompt us forth to the noblest aims and endeavors. Aspirants for the best, they prick us forward to its attainment, the more successfully as our theories of life lift us above the planes of precedent and routine, whereon the senses

confine us, to the mount of vision and of renovating
ideas. Nor are these too lofty or too beautiful to be
unattainable. 'T is when practice strays wide and falls
below that they appear visionary and fall into disre-
pute. Only those who mount the summits command
the valleys at their base.

> "When we ourselves from our own selves do quit,
>   And each thing else, then an all-spreading love
> To the vast universe our soul doth fit,
>   Makes us half equal to all-seeing Jove;
> Our mighty wings, high-stretched, then clapping light,
> We brush the stars, and make them seem more bright."

Enthusiasm is essential to the successful attainment of any high endeavor; without which incentive
one is not sure of his equality to the humblest undertaking even. And he attempts little worth living for if
he expects completing his task in an ordinary life-time.
His translation is for the continuance of his work here
begun, but for whose completion time and opportunity
were all too narrow and brief. Himself is the success
or failure. Step by step one climbs the pinnacles of
excellence; life itself is but the stretch for that mountain of holiness. Opening here with humanity, 't is the
aiming at divinity in ever-ascending circles of aspiration
and endeavor. Who ceases to aspire, dies. Our pursuits are our prayers; our ideals our gods. And the
more persistent our endeavors to realize these, the less
distant they seem. They were not gods could we approach them at once. We were the atheists of our

senses without them. All of beauty and of beatitude
we conceive and strive for, ourselves are to be sometime.
Man becomes godlike as he strives for divinity, and
divinity ever stoops to put on humanity and deify mankind. Character is mythical. The excellent are unap-
proachable save by like excellence. A person every
way intelligible falls short of our conception of greatness ; he ceases to be great in our eyes. God is not
God in virtue of attributes, but of the mystery surrounding these. Could we see through the cloud that
envelopes our apprehensions, he were here, and ourselves
apparent in his likeness. "God," says Plato, "is in-
effable, hard to be defined, and having been discovered,
to make fully known."

> "He is above the sphere of our esteem,
>   And is best known in not defining him."

Any attempted definition would include whatsoever
is embraced within our notion of Personality, — would
exhaust our knowledge of nature and of ourselves.
Only as we become One Personally with Him do we
know Him and partake of his attributes.

"In the soul of man," says Berkeley, "prior and
superior to intellect, there is a somewhat of a higher
nature, by virtue of which we are ONE, and by means of
which we are most clearly joined to the Deity. And as
by our intellect we touch the divine intellect, even so
by our oneness, 'the very flower of our essence,' as
Proclus expresses it, we touch the First One. Exist

ence and One are the same. And consequently, our minds participate so far of existence as they do of unity. But it should seem the personality is the indivisible centre of the soul, or mind, which is a monad, so far forth as she is a person. Therefore Person is really that which exists, inasmuch as it partakes of the divine unity. Number is no object of sense, but an act of the mind. The same thing in a different conception is one or many. Comprehending God and the creatures in one general notion, we may say that all things together make one universe. But if we should say that all things make one God, this would indeed be an erroneous notion of God, but would not amount to atheism, so long as mind, or intellect, was admitted to be the governing part. It is, nevertheless, more respectful, and consequently the truer notion of God, to suppose Him neither made up of parts, nor himself to be a part of any whole whatsoever."

THE SEARCH AFTER GOD.*

"I sought Thee round about, O thou my God!
　　In thine abode,
I said unto the earth, 'Speak, art thou He?'
　　She answered me,
'I am not.' I inquired of creatures all
　　In general
Contained therein; they with one voice proclaim
That none amongst them challenged such a name.

* By Thomas Heywood, 1590.

"I asked the seas and all the deeps below,
  My God to know;
I asked the reptiles and whatever is
  In the abyss;
Even from the shrimp to the leviathan
  Inquiry ran, —
But in those deserts which no line can sound,
The God I sought for was not to be found.

"I asked the air if that were He? but, lo,
  It told me, No.
I from the towering eagle to the wren
  Demanded then
If any feathered fowl 'mongst them were such?
  But they all, much
Offended with my question, in full choir
Answered, 'To find thy God thou must look higher.

"I asked the heavens, sun, moon and stars; but they
  Said, 'We obey
The God thou seek'st.'   I asked what eye or ear
  Could see or hear;
What in the world I might descry or know
  Above, below?
With an unanimous voice, all these things said,
'We are not God, but we by Him were made.'

"I asked the world's great universal mass
  If that God was?
Which with a mighty and strong voice replied
  As stupefied,
'I am not He, O man! for know that I
  By Him on high
Was fashioned first of nothing, thus inflated,
And swayed by Him by whom I was created.'

" I sought the court, but smooth-tongued flattery there
   Deceived each ear :
 In the thronged city there was selling, buying,
   Swearing and lying, —
 In the country, craft in simpleness arrayed ;
   And then I said,
 ' Vain is my search, although my pains be great,
 Where my God is there can be no deceit.'

" A scrutiny within myself I then
   Even thus began :
 ' O man, what art thou ? ' What more could I say,
   Than dust and clay ?
 Frail mortal, fading, a mere puff, a blast
   That cannot last, —
 Enthroned to-day, to-morrow in an urn,
 Formed from that earth to which I must return.

" I asked myself, what this great God might be
   That fashioned me ?
 I answered, the all-potent, solely immense,
   Surpassing sense,
 Unspeakable, inscrutable, eternal,
   Lord over all ;
 The only terrible, strong, just and true,
 Who hath no end, and no beginning knew.

" He is the well of life, for He doth give
   To all that live
 Both breath and being ; he is the Creator
   Both of the water,
 Earth, air and fire ; of all things that subsist,
   He hath the list ;
 Of all the heavenly host, or what earth claims,
 He keeps the scroll, and calls them by their names.

" And now, my God, by thine illumining grace,
  Thy glorious face   .
 (So far forth as it may discovered be)
  Methinks I see;
 And though invisible and infinite
  To human sight,
 Thou in thy mercy, justice, truth, appearest,
 In which to our weak senses thou com'st nearest.

" O, make us apt to seek and quick to find
  Thou God most kind!
 Give us love, hope, and faith in thee to trust,
  Thou God most just!
 Remit all our offences, we entreat,
  Most Good, most Great!
 Grant that our willing, though unworthy quest,
 May through thy grace admit us 'mongst the blest."